POLITICS:

Who

Gets

What,

When,

How

POLITICS:

WHO
GETS
WHAT,
WHEN,
HOW

WITHDRAWN

by HAROLD D. LASSWELL

wright

With Postscript (1958)

A MERIDIAN BOOK

WORLD PUBLISHING

TIMES MIRROR

NEW YORK

A MERIDIAN BOOK

Published by The World Publishing Company
110 East 59th Street, New York, New York 10022
First Meridian printing September 1958
Twelfth printing 1972
Postscript (1958) copyright © 1958 by The World Publishing
Company; copyright © 1951 by The Free Press in its volume
The Political Writings of Harold D. Lasswell; copyright ©
1936 by McGraw-Hill Book Company.
Reprinted by arrangement with The Free Press of Glencoe.
Library of Congress Catalog Card Number: 58-11925
ISBN 0-529-02106-4
Printed in the United States of America.

WORLD PUBLISHING
TIMES MIRROR

269579

JA
73
.L3
1958

CONTENTS

PREFACE

The interpretation of politics found in this book underlies the working attitude of practicing politicians. One skill of the politician is calculating probable changes in influence and the influential.

This version of politics is not novel to all students of social development. Yet it is constantly in danger of attenuation. Even now there is no brief book in English which states this standpoint for student, teacher, scholar, citizen, and politician, and which sees it in relation to passing time.

Certain practical and theoretical consequences follow from the lack of opportune reminders of this fundamental standpoint. That practicing politicians, caught in the immediate, lose sight of the remote, is to be expected. That systematic students, exempted from instant and overwhelming necessity, often grow precise about the trivial, need occasion no surprise.

Concepts for the study of influence must be changed or invented when influence is sought by novel means or under changed conditions. In epochs of rapid development, there is need to reassess the relevance of intellectual effort. Of the need for orientation in our day nearly everyone is convinced. A society newly devoted to planning may (as Karl Mannheim contends) require new styles of thought.

The spirit of critical discontent is rife in the world outside the Soviet Union. Well-built highroads of intellectual achievement are traveled with reluctance, not in protest against the engineering, but in skepticism of starting point and destination. Much of the literature of comparative government, law, and administration is devoted to the taxonomy of institutional practice, with little reference to the living forms which are thereby helped or hurt. The rude glare of political analysis is dimmed in the literature of political quietism.

British, Austrian, and American economics are not impervious to the intellectual weather. Classical economics, if we are to believe Ricardo, was concerned with the distribution of wealth, one of the principal means of influence. The conditions of wealth distribution under conditions of free competition have been carefully phrased. Distribution under other conditions was understressed in classical analysis. Modern events have sharply reminded us that distribution depends on myth and violence (on faith and brigandage) as well as bargaining.

Little more has been done in this book than to state and illustrate the standpoint. The connection between what is written here and what has been written elsewhere is to some extent shown in the bibliographic notes to the separate chapters which are printed at the end of the book. Specialists will be at no loss to distinguish between the original and the large body of derivative material. Those who accept the frame of reference here proposed will share common standards to guide future intellectual effort.

There are many practical implications which follow

from various aspects of this analysis. My findings are in many respects parallel to the concluding chapters of *The Promise of American Politics* by my friend, colleague, and representative, Professor and State Senator T. V. Smith. This is most gratifying to me in every one of my capacities as friend, colleague, and constituent.

The quotation from *An Experiment in Autobiography,* published by The Macmillan Company, is by kind permission of H. G. Wells. The sentences from Eugene O'Neill's *Mourning Becomes Electra* are reprinted by courtesy of Random House.

H. D. L.

PART I: *Elite*

ONE

ELITE

The study of politics is the study of influence and the influential. The science of politics states conditions; the philosophy of politics justifies preferences. This book, restricted to political analysis, declares no preferences. It states conditions.

The influential are those who get the most of what there is to get. Available values may be classified as *deference, income, safety*. Those who get the most are *elite;* the rest are *mass*.

The distribution of deference is relatively clear in a formal hierarchy. The peak of the Roman Catholic pyramid is occupied by a comparatively small number of officials. There are one Pope, 55 cardinals, 22 apostolic delegates, 256 vicars apostolic, 245 archbishops, 1,578 bishops. The Communist party in the Soviet Union comes to a sharp head in the Political Committee of nine or ten members. The looser structure of government in the United States none the less confers special influence upon the Supreme Court of nine, the

Presidency of one, and the Congress of a few hundred. Although any bright and talkative lad in the United States may be told that one day he may be president, only eight boys made it in the last generation. The potent American Senate, though comparatively large, would provide a place for only 480 senators each generation were none reelected. Deference pyramids, in form and in fact, are steep.

The distribution of safety is usually less inequitable than the distribution of deference, and may often show a negative relationship to it. Thus one study showed that 31.9 per cent of a series of 423 monarchs of different countries and different periods died by violence. Forty per cent of the presidents of the Republic of Bolivia came to a violent end. Such figures may be put in rough perspective by recalling that deaths by violence (including suicide) in the United States were 7.2 per cent of the whole number of deaths in 1921; 12.1 per cent of the presidents of the United States and of France, and 9 per cent of the Catholic popes, died by violence. The relative safety of whole populations varies from epoch to epoch. Five of every thousand Frenchmen who died in the seventeenth century were killed or wounded in battle. The number rose to twelve in the eighteenth century, thirteen in the nineteenth, and fourteen in the twentieth.

In countries of Western European civilization wealth and income are inequitably distributed. In 1928, a year of great business and speculative activity, the national income of the United States was $541 per capita, which was two and a half times the figure for France or Germany (the dollar is quoted in terms of the purchasing power of 1913). In 1913, just before the World War, the figure had been $368 per capita in the United States. In the interim the United States showed the largest absolute increase among the major powers, but the sharpest relative advance was made by Japan, whose per capita rose from $22 in 1913 to $53 in 1925. The United Kingdom, next to the United

States in absolute numbers, stood at $250 in 1911 and $293 in 1928. Russia rose from $52 in 1914 to $96 in 1928, which was greater than the relative gain of France or Germany. Italy dropped from $108 in 1914 to $96 in 1928.

There are sharp differences in the apportionment of income within given communities. Ten per cent of the population of the United States took one-third of the money income of the nation in the years between 1918 and 1926.

The values of deference, safety, and income which have just been singled out are representative and not exclusive values. Political analysis could make use of other combinations, and the resulting elite comparisons would differ. The findings of political analysis also vary when different characteristics of the influential are chosen for emphasis. One form of analysis considers the division of values according to *skill*.

Fighting skill is plainly one of the most direct ways by which men have come to the top, whether the fighting be done in the name of god, nation, or class. Mustafa Kemal Pasha fought in the Turco-Italian War in 1911, and commanded the northern section of the Turkish army in Gallipoli in 1915, and elsewhere. Mussolini and Hitler got their baptism of fire in the World War. Several men at the helm in the Soviet Union made their way mainly by illegal, rather than legal, violence. Josef Stalin was first arrested in 1901 by the authorities, and thereafter went into hiding, worked in the revolutionary movement, and ran constant risks. Joseph Pilsudski, former dictator of Poland, banished to Siberia for his connection with the Polish national movement in 1888, joined the Socialist party in 1892, and organized secret military units.

Hermann Göring was the last commander of the "Freiherr von Richthofen" squadron, which made distinguished history in the last years of the World War. Rudolf Hess, National Socialist party secretary, and close associate of Hitler, was a former member of the

German scouting flight "35." Dr. Robert Ley, leader of the National Socialist trade unions, was a military airman, as was Gregor Strasser, who was so closely connected with Hitler until shortly before the Nazi's assumption of power. The same active role in partisan politics has often been assumed by naval officers, and particularly by submarine officers.

In connection with civil posts intimately associated with violence may be recalled the prescriptive right of the Roosevelt family to an assistant-secretaryship of the navy. Once there was Theodore Roosevelt; later Franklin D. Roosevelt served from 1913 to 1920, and was in charge of the inspection of United States naval forces in European waters, July-September, 1918.

Skill in political organization is traditionally represented in the American Cabinet by the postmaster general. Skill in organization was indispensable to the elimination of Trotsky by Communist party secretary Stalin. Hitler is a notable combination of oratory and organization; Mussolini, of oratory, journalism, and organization; Masaryk, of oratory, journalism, scholarship, and organization. It is noteworthy that the political committee of the Communist party has gradually altered its composition, substituting more skill in organization for skill in oratory, journalism, and scholarship.

Skill in handling persons by means of sigificant symbols involves the use of such media as the oration, the polemical article, the news story, the legal brief, the theological argument, the novel with a purpose, and the philosophical system. The opportunities for men to live by manipulating symbols have grown apace with the complication of our material environment through the expansion of technology. Since 1870, for example, professional authors in America have jumped from an inconsequential number to between 12,000 and 13,000. There are 60,000 artists where formerly there were 4,000; 40,000 actors instead of 2,000; 165,000 muscians in place of 16,000. There has been a tenfold increase in the teaching profession. There are ten newspapermen where there was one in 1870. There are 300,000 lawyers today; and it is common knowledge how much influence is exercised by lawyers in courts, legislatures, commissions, and on boards of directors. Half of the President's Cabinet are lawyers.

Specialists on the handling of things, as well as persons, have spectacularly increased in modern times. In the United States technical engineers (excluding electricians) have risen from 7,000 in 1870 to over 226,000 in 1930 (the gainfully employed as a whole expanded only 300 per cent). Yet those who specialize in engineering receive less deference than those who specialize in symbols which sway the masses.

It was skill in bargaining that was the road to eminence as modern industry expanded during the nineteenth and twentieth centuries.

Elites may be compared in terms of *class* as well as skill. A class is a major social group of similar function, status, and outlook. The principal class formations in recent world politics have been aristocracy, plutocracy, middle class, and manual toilers.

In 1925 the landed aristocracy of Germany owned most of the large estates which occupied 20.2 per cent of the arable land of the country. They had 40 per cent of the land east of the Elbe River. All told, these large estates constituted but 0.4 per cent of the total number of landholdings in Germany. At the base of the pyramid were those who occupied small holdings: 59.4 per cent of the total holdings of Germany accounted for only 6.2 per cent of the arable land.

The concentration of landownership in the hands of a small aristocratic coterie is especially noteworthy in Chile, where it has been officially estimated that 2,500 individuals hold 50,000,000 acres of the 57,000,000 acres in private possession. In prewar Hungary properties of 1,300 acres or more, comprising only one-tenth of one per cent of the total number of holdings in the country, included 17.5 per cent of the total area. So large were the holdings of the aristocracy in the Baltic provinces of the former Russian Empire that a new state like Estonia found at the beginning of its national life that 1,149 large estates occupied 58 per cent of its total area. In Latvia, where one-half of the country was in 1,300 baronical estates, land reforms created 43,000 new peasant holdings by 1922.

Great plutocracies have arisen from commerce, industry, and finance, as capitalistic society developed through its several phases. Typical of the merchant capitalist period was the fortune of John Jacob Astor, which aggregated $20,000,000 and was derived from the oriental and fur trade, and from speculation in New York real estate. Industrial fortunes rose later. Cornelius Vanderbilt left $100,000,000 from speculations in railroads. Cyrus McCormick built on the basis of agricultural machinery, Andrew Carnegie on steel, John D. Rockefeller on oil, and J. Pierpont Morgan on investment banking. By 1929 there were 504 persons in America whose incomes were in excess of $1,000,000, and whose wealth was $35,000,000,000. As a rule these great fortunes were highly diversified, representing paper control over remote operations.

At the end of the eighteenth century the rising bourgeoisie clashed sharply with the French aristocracy, but elsewhere the new bourgeoisie fused more readily with the declining aristocracy. Although the largest fortune in Germany in 1913 was the Krupp fortune of $70,000,000, representing the new industrial capitalists, the second largest fortune was owned by the aristocrat Prince Henckel von Donnersmarck. The Kaiser was fifth. Most of the aristocratic fortunes had become diversified and depended upon typically capitalistic undertakings.

The gradualness of the eclipse of the aristocracy by new social formations is indicated by the analysis of British Cabinet ministers since the beginning of the nineteenth century. Harold J. Laski has shown that between 1801 and 1831 no less than 52 of the 71 ministers of Cabinet rank were sons of nobility. Between 1906 and 1916 the sons of nobility sank to parity with other social classes, contributing 25 of the 51 ministers. From 1917 to 1924 but 14 of the 53 ministers were from the nobility.

In Japan the transition to modern industrialism and finance was managed by parceling the new enterprises among the great feudal families.

The lesser middle class is composed of those who exercise skills which are requited by modest money returns. Hence the class comprises small farmers, small businessmen, low-salaried professional people, skilled workers and craftsmen. The manual workers are those who have acquired little skill; they are the true proletariat. The line between plutocracy, lesser bourgeoisie, and proletariat is a matter of acrimonious debate in practical politics, and of great uncertainty among scientists. Socialist propagandists have sometimes sought to include skilled workers, and even low-income professional people, among the proletariat. Propagandists of plutocracy have sought to obscure the demarcation between big business and big finance, on the one hand, and lesser business and lesser finance, on the other, by speaking of "business" as a unit.

Arthur N. Holcombe applied the terms defined by Bukharin to the United States with these results: by assigning 24,800,000 of the gainfully employed and 14,000,000 female homemakers to the "proletariat," he arrived at a figure for the "proletariat" which was 51.7 per cent of the gainfully employed; 1.6 per cent were "capitalists"; 8 per cent were "landlords"; the rest were "intermediate," "transitional," "mixed," and "unclassified." W. I. King estimated the average income of each person gainfully employed in the United States during 1924-1927 at $1,885. A substantial, though undetermined proportion, of the "proletariat" received more than this average amount.

There is an inner psychological attitude in common

among those who make sacrifices to acquire skill, and this bond tends to keep the lesser bourgeoisie identified with the plutocracy rather than with the skill-less proletariat. Common resentment against a social order which does not invariably apportion high rewards to skill draws the small professional man, businessman, farmer, and skilled worker away from the social forms which preserve plutocracy. Those who are classed as "proletariat" in the Holcombe analysis are skilled as well as semiskilled and unskilled; hence many of them belong to the lesser bourgeoisie as here understood. There is evidence that the white-collar worker and the professional man have been supplanting the muscle man in American life. It is estimated that the machine revolution has released about 25 per cent of all the working population of the United States from arduous toil, and labor-saving machinery has lightened the physical burdens of those who remain on farms and in mines and factories. In 1870 there were 52.8 per cent of the gainfully employed in agriculture. By 1930 this had declined to 21.3 per cent. Most of the change occurred in trade and transportation (rising from 9.1 to 20.7 per cent), clerical service (1.7 to 8.2 per cent), and professional service (2.7 to 6.5 per cent).

The distribution of values may be considered with reference to *personality* in addition to skill and class. What is the relative success of all the forms of personality known to clinical and cultural psychologists? What is the varying fortune of the masochists, the sadists, the detached, the hysterical, the obsessive, the compulsive? From this standpoint the march of time ceases to pivot exclusively around the cavalcade of classes and skills; it becomes a succession of personality forms.

Special interest attaches to personality forms which are predisposed by nature and by early nurture to find satisfaction in playing particular roles on the stage of politics. The agitator is such a type: he is set off from his fellows by the intensity of his craving for prompt and excited deference from his contemporaries. Hence he is emotionally disposed to cultivate such skills of mass appeal as oratory and polemical journalism. Men with less need for emotional responsiveness may be less spectacular organizers. The agitator comes into his own during the fiery intensity of crises; the organizer is favored by the intercrisis periods. As crises intensify, Asquith gives way to Lloyd George; von Hindenburg to Hitler. As crises relax, the stage is set for Stanley Baldwin or Warren Harding.

During the initial phases of crisis, personalities may forge ahead who are benevolent as well as firm, and more considerate than ruthless. The stern cloud of approaching war or revolution generates profound anxieties among the masses. The need for reassurance may favor the gentle Lincoln over the flaming Seward on the very eve of disaster.

There are forms of personality easily addicted to imperious violence. They have often learned to cow their environment by the sheer intensity of their willfulness. They have succeeded in control by externalizing their rages against deprivation. Such are the men of Napoleonic mold, prone to break themselves or others.

Whatever the special form of political expression, the common trait of the political personality type is emphatic demand for deference. When such a motive is associated with skill in manipulation, and with timely circumstances, an effective politician is the result. The fully developed political type works out his destiny in the world of public objects in the name of public good. He displaces private motives on public objects in the name of collective advantage.

The true political personality is a complex achievement. When infants are born, they are unequipped with language of reference to environment, immediate or remote. Their impulses are first organized toward an immediate intimate circle. The symbols of reference to the world of affairs are endowed with meaning in this primary situation, and the true politician learns to use the world of public objects as a means of alleviating the stresses of his intimate environment. Cravings for deference, frustrated or overindulged in the intimate circle, find expression in the secondary environment. This displacement is legitimized in the name of plausible symbols. He does not act for the sake of action; he implies that he strives for the glory of God, the sanctity of the Home, the independence of the Nation, the emancipation of the Class. In the extreme case, the politician is bound to no specific objects in his environment. He is not preoccupied with the routines of nature, discernible in science, art, technology; he is concerned only with the deference meaning of objects for his ego.

Besides skill, classes, and personality groups, we may examine the distribution of values among *attitude groups*. The world is divided among those who are influential on the basis of shared symbols of loyalty to nation, class, occupation, person. Some rise to eminence in the name of militant or conciliatory methods; in the name of demands for a vast gamut of policies; in the name of optimistic visions of the future. Quite different personality types may be united in loyalty to nation or class, method, policy, outlook. Thus attitude groups cut across personality classifications, even as they cut across skill or class. At any given time the members of a skill or class group may not have risen to full skill or class consciousness. Although an objective observer may be able to consider the meaning of events for their relative success or failure, the members of the skill or class group may talk the language of patriotism, and have no common symbol of class or skill.

At this point it may be convenient to cast a glance backward over the ground which has been covered. The term politics has been used to mean the study of influence and the influential. It is plain, however, that no simple index can be profitably used to measure influence and the influential. One aspect of influence is the relative sharing of values. Different results can be obtained by using different values. *An* elite of deference is not necessarily *an* elite of safety. More values may be added to the present list of three (deference, safety, income). Whatever the list, the items may be differently combined, thus reaching different results to correspond to varying judgments of *the* elite. New results may be obtained by defining influence in other terms than relative share of values. The term may be used to indicate a judgment of how values *might* be influenced if there were conflicts about them. Thus financial capitalists may be judged to be stronger or weaker than industrial capitalists in case of a hypothetical collision.

From analysis, then, we can expect no static certainty. It is a constant process of reexamination which brings new aspects of the world into the focus of critical attention. The unifying frame of reference for the special student of politics is the rich and variable meaning of "influence and the influential," "power and the powerful."

Perhaps the reader may find himself pausing to consider his own position in the world from the standpoints thus far developed. What is my principal skill? What is my class? What is my type of personality? What are my loyalties and my preferences about collective policy and attitude? Where do these skill, class, and personality formations stand with reference to the distribution of such values as deference, safety, and income in my locality, my region my state, my continent, my world? How has my position altered so far during my life, and what are the probable alterations before I die?

Plainly the last question poses the most crucial problem in the sharpest possible way. One purpose of thought is to help in locating the self as an object among objects in the march of time. The goal is to view the self correctly in the context of events which include the future as well as the past. In this case, the objective is orientation in the succession of skill, class, personality, and attitude forms through time.

This is the *contemplative* approach to political events. But there is a *manipulative* approach as well. It views events in order to discover ways and means of gaining goals. Such a standpoint does not necessarily call for overt participation in revolutionary or counterrevolutionary, reformist or counterreformist movements, although it does bring the attitude of the analyst much closer to that of the agitator-organizer. If events are viewed in this perspective, a new sense of personal involvement may have a vitalizing effect upon the thinker when he resumes the contemplative attitude.

How may elites be attacked or defended? How may specific objectives be reached by means of symbols, violence, goods, practices? Such are the major problems of the manipulative approach to politics as here understood; such are the questions to be broached in the next four chapters. The contemplative approach is then resumed, and the meaning of events is construed with reference to skill, class, personality, attitude.

It may be serviceable to put the present interpretation of politics in the perspective of recent specialized thought on the subject. Not until 1906 were there enough political scientists in the United States to organize a national organization (although the American Economic Association was founded in 1885). The original members of the association were recruited from the faculties or departments of government or political science, and from some departments of history and philosophy, and from some schools of law. Although these political scientists had different technical skills at their command, they were united by common interest in what was understood to be the institution of government. As distinguished from law and philosophy, political science was chiefly comparative government, emphasizing the broad historical transformations which ushered in modern institutions, especially in Western Europe and in English-speaking countries.

In recent years, academic political science has enlarged its descriptive content by concentrating attention upon public administration, political parties, promotional groups, and political personalities. Political scientists have become more preoccupied with the recent past and the impending future than with the remote past. One result of this shift in focus of attention has been the use of methods of investigation which were not included in the traditional equipment of historians, philosophers, and lawyers.

The study of the recent past and the impending future drew attention to the techniques of the interview and of field observation. This brought more political scientists into contact with specialists who were skilled in interviewing primitive people (cultural anthropologists), in eliciting life history documents (social psychologists, sociologists), in prolonged and technical interviewing (clinical psychology, notably psychoanalysis), and in controlled observation (behavioristic psychology, child psychology, applied psychology).

Preoccupied with the recent past and the impending future, political scientists have studied classes of recurring events (like voting). This made it possible to compare results by the use of quantitative procedures, and brought political scientists into more intimate contact with statisticians.

Thus it was not to the historian, the lawyer, or the philosopher that the political scientist was able to turn for aid in the solution of his problems, but to the new and growing skill groups in the academic division of labor.

Plainly such changes in outlook were likely to work changes in the concepts, as well as in the techniques, of political scientists. Some became discontented with the identification of their field with "government" or the "state." They found that the traditional vocabulary of political science was not easily adapted to the statement of relative changes. The traditional distinctions were between "sovereign" and "not sovereign," "state" and "not state," "centralized" and "decentralized." But most events seemed to fall somewhere between these "either-or" words, and to demand language capable of distinguishing between "more or less." Prolonged research might result in classifying the states of the world into "dictatorships" or "nondictatorships," but the two-term classification did not seem to be particularly important. Hence the growing interest in varying degrees of "power" or "influence," and in the use of tentative and partial indicators of influence.

That political science concentrates upon the influential does not imply the neglect of the total distribution of values throughout the community. It is impossible to locate the few without considering the many. And the emphasis upon the probability that the few will get the most does not imply that the many do not profit from some political changes.

Moreover, the analysis of political results in terms of certain values (like deference, safety, income) does not imply that the results or the values are consciously sought. It is a matter of investigation to determine the influence of self-conscious striving. "Class consequences" and "skill consequences" may, in some circumstances, come to pass with a mere modicum of "class consciousness" and "skill consciousness." The subjective attitudes actually found may damage rather than improve the relative influence of class or skill groups. Such attitudes would be "false class (or skill) consciousness," rather than "true class (or skill) consciousness."

Political science, then, is the study of influence and the influential. Influence is determined on the basis of shares in the values which are chosen for purposes of the analysis. Representative values are deference, safety, and income. No single index is wholly satisfactory as a gauge of influence, but situations may be clarified by the successive application of specific standards. Whatever the measures utilized, attention is centered upon the characteristics of the influential which may be described in selected terms, like class, skill, personality, and attitude. The fate of an elite is profoundly affected by the ways it manipulates the environment; that is to say, by the use of violence, goods, symbols, practices.

This book will begin with the methods *of* the influential, and conclude with the consequences *for* the influential.

PART II: *Methods*

TWO

SYMBOLS

Any elite defends and asserts itself in the name of symbols of the common destiny. Such symbols are the "ideology" of the established order, the "utopia" of counter-elites. By the use of sanctioned words and gestures the elite elicits blood, work, taxes, applause, from the masses. When the political order works smoothly, the masses venerate the symbols; the elite, self-righteous and unafraid, suffers from no withering sense of immorality. "God's in his heaven—all's right with the world." "In union there is strength"—not exploitation.

A well-established ideology perpetuates itself with little planned propaganda by those whom it benefits most. When thought is taken about ways and means of sowing conviction, conviction has already languished, the basic outlook of society has decayed, or a new, triumphant outlook has not yet gripped the automatic loyalties of old and young. Happy indeed is that nation that has no thought of itself; or happy at least are the few who procure the principal benefits of universal

31

acquiescence. Systems of life which confer special benefits on the other fellow need no plots or conspiracies when the masses are moved by faith and the elites are inspired by self-confidence.

Any well-knit way of life molds human behavior into its own design. The individualism of bourgeois society like the communism of a socialized state must be inculcated from the nursery to the grave. In the United States, as one among the bourgeois nations, the life of personal achievement and personal responsibility is extolled in song and story from the very beginning of consciousness. Penny banks instill the habit of thrift; trading in the schoolyard propagates the bourgeois scale of values. Individual marks at school set the person at rivalrous odds with his fellows. "Success and failure depend on you." "Strive and succeed" means "If you strive, success comes; if success does not come, you have not striven hard enough."

"The almighty dollar": money is scarce and "it is not wise to buy the bicycle now"; "we must be economical and keep the old car another season"; "they're headed for the poorhouse; have you seen how she dresses!"; "they were worthy people, but she's a shame and a disgrace to her parents"; "they had a falling out over the will"; "she really married him for his money"; "some say he poisoned her so he could collect the insurance"; "he was a brilliant man but he took to drink and went to the dogs"; "he was a good provider until he went running around spending his money on loose women"; "I hear Harry is making a good thing of it in real estate"; "how much did that cost you?"; "how much is the tuition at that college?"

The rich and successful uncle, the rich and successful deacon, the rich and successful alumnus, the rich and successful banker are there at the focus of adulation. Their portraits ornament the walls; their busts adorn the halls; their presences dignify occasions. Epithets are passed around the dinner table or the nursery or the street corner when "failures" beg for charity, or resort to theft or worse.

Gossip, fiction, motion pictures sustain the thesis of personal responsibility for failure or success. He failed because he lacked tact or had halitosis or didn't finish his education by correspondence or didn't go to the right college or forgot to slick down his hair. She was successful because she got the right shade of lipstick, took French lessons at home on the phonograph, kept the skin you love to touch, and bought soft and subtle kinds of lingerie. If she took up typewriting and short-hand, she would marry the boss. Not untypical of the sudden success motifs are the following motion pictures seen in succession by a movie addict: In "I'm No Angel" the ex-carnival girl marries a society man. In "Morning Glory" a stage-struck country girl is shoved into the star part on the opening night of a play and makes a hit. In "My Weakness" a servant girl made into a lady wins a society man. In "Emperor Jones" a negro porter rises to kingly heights before he fails. In "Footlight Parade" a young producer makes good with one night of strenuous work.

Social and industrial difficulties are automatically traced to personal equations. If conditions are wretched at the X Company coal mine, it is because the owners back in New York didn't know about it. Meanwhile trouble may be made by radical agitators or by racketeers, who stir up the men in order to get themselves employed as strike leaders or as strike-breakers.

The focus of attention is thus absorbed by personal problems. The newspapers report that he killed her because he found her with another man, or because she could not see him go to another woman. The newspapers report that he won an election because he made a smart speech. The newspapers report that he got killed because he forgot to look to see if the train was coming. The newspapers report that she got hurt because she did not read the instructions on the package. The particular incident is not written about as representative of a context of relationships. Not desperation through unemployment, not insecurity through crop failure, not diminished administrative efficiency because of greater burdens of prohibitory regulation, but personal motives and struggles are the subject matter of the secondary means of communication in the bourgeois world.

When such an ideology impregnates life from start to finish, the thesis of collective responsibility runs against a wall of noncomprehension. In any collective society, the whole texture of life experience would need to be respun. In the Soviet Union, for instance, there have been efforts to remodel the psychological environment of the rising generation. This has meant collective houses, where community laundries and similar services replace the private unit. Group tasks supplant individual tasks in order to keep collective enterprises rather than ambitious persons at the center of attention. Theatricals emphasize the play and not the star, and treat the fate of movements rather than the problems of the individual person.

The emblems and words of the organized community are also part of the precious haze of early experience. In the United States the memories of all are entwined with the flag, snapping in the breeze on Memorial Day; "The Star-Spangled Banner," sung in uncertain unison on special holidays; the oath of allegiance to the flag repeated before hours of study and recitation; the pageant of the Pilgrim Fathers, rehearsed at school, at church, at club. There are memories of stiff, embarrassed silence at the name of the slacker relative; tales of travel and adventure with the fleet, the army, the air force; solemn requiem for the dead; marching columns of the gray, blue, khaki.

On occasions like the inauguration of the President, the unifying symbols of the nation rise again to the threshold of attention. The identifying term has changed from time to time. Before the Civil War, this was the "Union," but the bloody and contentious associations of that word led to its practical elimination in presidential rhetoric after the Civil War. The term "United States" has been dropping out to the advantage of "America" or "American," notably since the World War. Inaugural oratory has invariably contained reference to the deity, and usually to words like "freedom," "liberty," "independence," "economy," "self-government." Even George Washington made an allusion to the common past, and after Franklin Pierce "our glorious past" or "our memories" were duly celebrated. Such expressions as "our fathers, our forefathers, the framers, the founders, our sages, heroes" were seldom left out. "Confidence in the future" was omitted by James Monroe and Grover Cleveland only. Adverse references were made to "partisanship" in most of the addresses. Usually there were self-adulatory words like "intelligence of our people, our righteous people, our great nation."

In the picture language of the public, reflected in cartoons, foreign nations have often played a sorry role, except when public sympathy moved more or less episodically in their favor. For many years the "Mexican" stereotype included a bolero coat, a large sombrero, spurs, revolver, and rifle. The clothes were often torn and ragged, with patched shoes or bare feet. The dark hair, slightly upturned mustache, dark eyes, clenched fist, defiant face aroused annoyance rather than hatred. The "Mexican" was often shown as a small, thin urchin who should be soundly spanked and put to bed. Sometimes he was depicted as playing with fire, or sticking his tongue out at Uncle Sam, or being caught in a juvenile prank by his policeman neighbor to the north.

Before 1915 there was some uncertainty about the stereotype of the "Japanese." He figured as a little boy or as a tiny man wearing a kimono. As late as May, 1915, the cartoonist Bowers drew the "Japanese" with a kimono reaching to the knees, big bow tie at the back, bare arms and legs, shaven head, row of white teeth, and spear in hand. But in 1915 the tendency was to discard the kimono and array the "Jap" in a military outfit, usually a short plain coat (minus decorations), trousers, tight-fitting military boots, military cap, sword, and often a revolver or bayonet. Occasionally, especially at the era of the Washington Conference, the "Jap" was portrayed in an ordinary business suit; but by 1925 he was back in full military regalia.

The bias against government is strikingly indicated by the absence of a cartoon stereotype for the public as a recipient of benefits from public expenditures. The emphasis is all on the "Taxpayer." Often arrayed in a dark suit with a white collar, four-in-hand tie, sometimes with a white vest, often with light trousers, the taxpayer is one of those pathetic souls who always gets it in the neck. Formerly equipped with straw hat, derby, or large cowboy hat, he is now more commonly shown in a soft felt hat of varying size, sometimes perched on top of his head, sometimes plopped down over his ears. Shoes may be ragged and patched, but the white collar of respectability remains. The frail little fellow has thinning hair, a long nose, a slight mustache, and glasses. The nosepinchers were replaced by horn-rims about 1921. The "Taxpayer," unlike the "Public," is always being acted upon. He may be an Isaac about to be sacrificed; a bandaged cripple leaving the office of Doc. Democrat to get relief from Doc. G.O.P.; a rower, trying to row five large cruisers to the scrap heap; a sawhorse, on which governmental extravagances and waste are teeter-tottering.

Singularly enough, the stereotype of the "Capitalist" has remained uncomplimentary for many years. The checkered trousers with dark coat and checkered suit tended to give way in 1910 and 1911 to the dark suit or a dark coat and striped trousers. The white vest, winged collar, bow tie (or four-in-hand), stovepipe hat, varying in size and weight, have long been consistently included within the stereotype. The amount of jewelry varies. At times he is bedecked with diamond studs, or a stickpin, cuff links, and diamond rings, even on thumb and first finger. Spats were added to his attire around 1912 and 1913, and his shiny patent leather shoes have been fixtures. Big cigars and a big cane are sometimes added. The "Capitalist" is fat necked, round bellied, and bald. The hands at times are excessively large to emphasize the grasping habits of the owner. Most of the time the "Capitalist" has been grinning, or smiling, at the expense of "Laborer" or "Public." But in the years 1919-1921 the negative symbol was that of "Labor" who was decked out with silk shirts and arrogance.

When elites resort to propaganda, the tactical problem is to select symbols and channels capable of eliciting the desired concerted acts. There is incessant resort to repetition or distraction. The changing emotional requirements of the community, moods of submissiveness, moods of self-assertion, all complicate the task of managing men in the mass. After periods of discipline for the common cause, the mass trend is toward individualism and variety; after periods of self-assertion, the mass trend is toward disciplined fundamentalism. This means that when the mores are observed, the countermores are suppressed; that when countermores are indulged, mores are suppressed. The inhibited is not extinct; hence the sudden change in direction which distinguishes the variable moods of men.

Propaganda, when successful, is astute in handling:

> Aggressiveness
> Guilt
> Weakness
> Affection.

The organization of the community for war takes advantage of the concentrated aggressiveness which accumulates in any crisis. When another nation is presented as a threat, retaliatory impulses to destroy it are promptly evoked; but such impulses cannot find direct expression. They are partially suppressed, partially repressed, but they contribute to the trend and tone of mental life. The energy of frustrated impulses may be discharged in many paths, but men in the mass are likely to use the most primitive. One of the rudimentary modes of coping with internal stress is projection. This mechanism resolves the inner emotional difficulties by treating an impulse of the self as an attribute of the environment. Instead of recognizing the simple intensity of one's retaliatory destructiveness, one feels that the outside world is more destructive than in reality it is. This "moralizes" the murderous impulse by imputing destructiveness to the other fellow. The symbol of the "other" is elaborated into a scheming, treacherous, malevolent "influence."

Deep-seated guilt feelings can also be projected upon the world outside. Hostile impulses arouse guilt feelings because society has taught the individual during infancy, childhood, and juvenility to chasten his rages. The initial tendency to hold the destructive tendencies in check by raging against the self can be dealt with by projecting the accusation away from the self, and raging at the "immorality" of the enemy.

Intense inner rage arouses deep fears of death and mutilation. (In part these are the "castration anxieties" spoken of in technical psychoanalysis.) Such fears of being hopelessly weakened, of enduring the humiliation of inferiority now and in the future, may also be assuaged by projection. Not ourselves, but our enemies, face defeat; our victory is sure.

As crisis grows, the "nation" is constantly kept at the focus of attention. The recurring preoccupations of everyday life are modified by news and rumors of international friction. All eyes focus upon the fate of the national "we" symbol in relation to the surrounding "they" symbols. Love and respect for the symbols of the foreigner are withdrawn and become attached to symbols of the collective "we." The sense of being threatened increases the need for love; hence the symbol of the nation is redefined as infinitely protective and indulgent, powerful and wise.

When war propaganda is addressed to the neutrals, the task is to lead influential elements in the neutral state to identify our enemy as their enemy, our cause as their cause. This can be accomplished by affording active opportunities for observers to become participants. Thus the cause of the Entente in the United States benefited from the charity drives to "adopt an orphan" from the devastated regions of "bleeding Belgium." British propaganda in America, 1914-1917, was wise in that so much of it was secretly or privately managed. It used the personal touch, and depended on American personnel and material wherever possible. Some of the German agents permitted themselves to become conspicuous; hence they were discredited. As a reminder of the ancient history of propaganda, it may be remarked that one of the plays of Euripides was probably a propaganda drama written to influence Argos against Sparta. The play was first produced, not at Athens, but at Argos; Peleus, it will be recalled, indulges in disparaging remarks about the Lacedaemonian women.

When the propaganda problem is to deal with allies, the cardinal themes are our strenuous exertions in the war and our hearty support of the cherished war aims of our allies.

The principal goal of propaganda in enemy countries is to deflect animosity against another foe, or to turn this animosity inward, thus fomenting civil war or revolution. The connection between fluctuating levels of insecurity and the effectiveness of propaganda is shown in the history of German morale during the World War. After the check on the Marne and the immobile war of the trenches, the bubbling self-confidence and enthusiasm at the front and at home began to subside. The glorious march to Paris had not come off. The simpler soldiers yearned to get out of the trenches by Christmas. But it was not until the food shortage pinched the population at home that waves of discontent assumed significant proportions. In October, 1915, the chief of the Foreign Office press section noticed that complaints from wives at home were affecting morale at the front. In the summer of 1916, the letters home began to reflect the impact of the terrific losses around Verdun. The word *Schwindel* began to be used to refer to the war. The Somme created the impression that Allied resources of men and material were inexhaustible. A critical, carping spirit began to show itself, and the gap between officers and men began visibly to widen. The privations of the "turnip winter" of 1916-1917 augmented the depression at home. In the summer of 1917 war aims were much discussed, and the blatant demands of the *Vaterlandspartei* for great annexations undermined the impression that the war was solely for defense. The soldiers at the front resented the high wages of the workers in the munitions factories, and the high profits of the munitions makers.

After three months of incessant struggle in Flanders, there was an appreciable increase in the number of losses by capture. This telltale indication of sagging morale spread apace as the war drew to an end. Disciplinary difficulties were sometimes extreme when troops were transferred from the eastern theater to the western "graveyard." Partly as a result of such evidence, the High Command decided to stake everything on the great offensive of 1918. As early as June, however, the troops were plainly disintegrating. By July difficulties were flagrant, as shown by leaves without permission, crimes of cowardice, and open defiance of orders. August was a month of general apathy, hopelessness, indifference. During the last months of the war from three-quarters of a million to a million men succeeded in withdrawing themselves from active combat, and many of those who stayed at the front engaged in passive resistance. Willing soldiers began to be called "strikebreakers" and "warprolongers" by their comrades.

Ludendorff first took note of the effects of enemy propaganda in the summer of 1917. During 1918 the menace of enemy propaganda was betrayed by the phrases of enemy origin which appeared in letters home from the front, and in conversations overheard on troop trains and reported by intelligence officers to the high command. Such words as "Prussian militarism," "Pan-German," "bloodthirsty Kaiser," and "Junker" were employed in the sense intended by Allied propagandists. Soldiers learned the word "Republic" because the French promised to give special consideration to all captives or deserters who shouted the word and surrendered. Radical socialist propaganda had revived at home, after some of the socialist leadership recovered from the abandonment of internationalism in 1914. In 1918 troops transferred from the eastern theater of war to the western front had often fraternized with the Bolshevik soldiers, and spread a revolutionary interpretation of the war.

Entente propaganda was hammering home the thesis of the ultimate defeat of Germany, and inciting a governmental, as distinguished from a social, revolution. In the famous "war without weapons" the use of leaflets reached spectacular proportions. All told, 65,-595,000 leaflets were snowed over the German lines. The French distributed 43,300,000, the British, 19,295,-000, and the Americans 3,000,000. The German high command tried to defend itself by offering a bounty to soldiers who would turn in these leaflets. One-sixteenth of the leaflets dropped by the Allies were actually handed to their officers by the German soldiers. The Germans also tried to coordinate special propaganda at home with a strong counteroffensive against the Allies. They spread 2,253,000 copies of the *Gazette des Ardennes* on the western front.

The object of revolution, like war, is to attain coercive predominance over the enemy as a means of working one's will with him. Revolutionary propaganda selects symbols which are calculated to detach the affections of the masses from the existing symbols of authority, to attach these affections to challenging symbols, and to direct hostilities toward existing symbols of authority. This is infinitely more complex than the psychological problem of war propaganda, since in war the destructive energies of the community are drained along familiar channels. Most of those who have a hand in revolution must face a crisis of conscience. Constituted authority perpetuates itself by shaping the consciences of those who are born within its sphere of control. Hence the great revolutions are in defiance of emotions which have been directed by nurses, teachers, guardians, and parents along "accredited" channels of expression. Revolutions are ruptures of conscience.

The psychological function of revolutionary propaganda, like war propaganda, is to control aggressiveness, guilt, weakness, affection. Marxism, for example, fosters the projection of aggressiveness by denouncing "capitalism" as predatory. Marxism fosters the projection of guilt by indicting capitalism as the root of the ills of war, poverty, misery, disease. Marxism favors the projection of love upon "socialism" and the "proletariat." Marxism facilitates the projection of weakness by asserting that capitalistic society is bound to decay, for it bears the seed of revolution in its bosom. Hence, as was said by this writer in another context, "Dialectical materialism is the reading of private preferences into universal history, the elevating of personal aspirations into cosmic necessities, the remoulding of the universe in the pattern of desire, the completion of the crippled self by the incorporation of the symbol of the whole. No competing symbolism rose to such heights of compulsive formulation."

Partial revolutionary movements are led by an elite

which fights to exterminate those who are associated with the latest world revolutionary movement. Such movements, like Italian Fascism and German National Socialism, are belligerently antialien and pronational. Regardless of how much they borrow in symbol or practice from the latest world revolutionary pattern, they conceal the theft, abominate the source.

The use of the "non-Aryan" as the unifying devil behind all the lesser devils of Marxism, Versailles, Weimar, Dawes Plan, is easy to understand. The same type of mass movement in Italy had not utilized the Jew; but several circumstances conspired to heighten the availability of the Jew as a target of demagoguery in Germany. An analysis of these factors will illustrate the function of symbols in relation to context.

There were few Jews in Germany: they were bankers, merchants, and professional people who were inclined to treat Jew-baiting with disdain. There was no proletarian bloc of Jews to create a pro-Jewish backfire among the working masses. In short, the Jews were so numerous that they could conveniently be hated; not so numerous that they could effectively retaliate. The solid background of traditional anti-Semitism could be retouched and exploited with impunity.

Anti-Semitism gave an opportunity to discharge hatred against the rich and successful without espousing the proletarian socialists. Not "capitalism" but "Jewish profiteering" was the festering sore. Some German Jews were well-known international bankers, affording a solid basis of common knowledge for the tissue of exaggeration built about their influence. Smaller business and professional men, and petty officials, could attack the "system" without "degrading" themselves to the level of the "proletariat."

Even middle-class hatred of the proletariat could be split by means of the Jewish symbol. Thus the workers who were sufficiently German to renounce "Jewish doctrine" could be tolerated; those who remained

Jewish and "Red" and "Marxist" could be destroyed.

Aristocratic hatred of the consequences of modern industrialism could be split by having recourse to the Jew. The undesirable features exhibited the effect of international Jewish finance, not the inherent traits of the system. Hence it became possible to cooperate with capitalistic elements, and to turn the rage generated by recent economic changes against the irrelevant scapegoat.

Anti-Semitism was a means of crippling professional competitors, especially in the relatively congested fields of medicine, law, philosophy, science, and journalism.

Anti-Semitism was also an important means of discharging the hatred of the villager against the urbanite. Smoldering conflicts between rural, lesser urban, and metropolitan communities persist in every culture. Cities are the home of the new and hence of the shocking, for the new is ever threatening the older codes of morals and manners and tastes. City types are prominent among the enemies of the mores, and the Jews were city types. Had not Freud invented psychoanalysis, scandalizing the bourgeoisie? Had not Magnus Hirschfeld come to the defense of deviational sexual types? Had not Jewish writers, actors, painters contributed to the subversive fads of "cultural Bolshevism"?

The stresses of war, blockade, inflation, and deflation had exacted a tremendous moral toll in Germany. Multitudes had succumbed to sexual and property "temptations"; hence they were predisposed toward "purification" to remove the heavy hand of conscience. For them the Jew was the sacrificial Isaac. Indeed, the whole nineteenth century had witnessed the growth of the secular cult of nationalism, furnishing a substitute for the fading appeal of established religion. This decline of piety, however, left legacies of guilt which could be expiated by attacking the Jew, traditional enemy of Christianity.

Plainly the Jew was available as the symbol which more than any other could be utilized as a target of irrelevant emotional drives. The hatred of the country for the city, of the aristocracy for the plutocracy, of the middle class for the manual toilers and the aristocracy and the plutocracy could be displaced upon the Jew. The frustrations of economic adversity and international humiliation, guilt from immorality, guilt from diminishing piety—these stresses within the lives of Germans were available to be exploited in political action.

Propaganda, then, is conducted with symbols which are utilized as far as possible by elite and counter-elite; but the intensity of collective emotions and the broad direction and distribution of collective acts are matters of the changing total context.

THREE

VIOLENCE

Violence, a major means of elite attack and defense, takes many forms. The number of men who have been permanently included in the armed forces of the world gives some indication of the place of violence in politics.

In the early Roman Empire the standing army had about 300,000 men, or three in every thousand persons. Undoubtedly this was the largest standing army of ancient times. In the thirteenth century, Europe is estimated to have had the same proportion of its population under arms, though dispersed in a swarm of tiny principalities. By the early seventeenth century, Europe regained a population equal to that of the Roman Empire, and expanded both in numbers and in proportion in the army. During the Napoleonic period France sometimes had ten in every thousand persons under arms, and before the end of the nineteenth century all peacetime establishments of the great powers had climbed to this Napoleonic peak. During the World War no less than one hundred in every thousand of population were in arms. By 1934 the standing armies of Europe were twice the relative size of the Roman armies under Augustus.

The length of wars has declined, however, and so has the proportion of war years to peace years, if expeditions against peoples of inferior technique are excluded from the count. In the seventeenth century the great European states were at war about 75 per cent of the time. In the eighteenth century the per cent is 50; in the nineteenth century, 25. Counting the lesser acts of hostility, the great powers have been fighting most of the time. "Even the United States," says Quincy Wright, "which has perhaps somewhat unjustifiably prided itself on its peacefulness, has had only twenty years during its entire history of 158 years when it has not had the army or navy in active operations during some days, somewhere."

Such impressive reminders cover but a fraction of acts of collective violence. A balance sheet of violence would add those killed in revolution and counterrevolution, in uprisings, in the administration of criminal justice. Specialists in violence include watchmen, guardsmen, and policemen, besides members of the naval, military, and aerial forces. It may be noted that in some communities, like Chicago, the number of policemen in private employ is estimated to outnumber the policemen in government service. A prisoner is deprived of liberty by means of legal action sanctioned by the coercive authority of the community, and the prison population of the United States rose faster than population increased, jumping from 67,000 in 1890 to 140,000 in 1930.

If we include those who practice the use of firearms and explosives, and who learn the manual of arms, the function of violence seems to be even more extensive than shown by the foregoing indices. And if we add the frequency with which violence is resorted to in private relationships which do not come to the cognizance of officials, we would arrive at stupendous figures.

Plainly the rational application of violence as an instrument of influence depends upon the clear appraisal of the act of violence as a detail of the total context. It is seldom an instrument of total destruction. It is a means to an end and not an end in itself. Yet so potent is the love of cruelty, whether in the form of direct gratification or in the indirect form of overreactive weakness, that the rational use of violence is beset by serious difficulties. As a precaution against the joys of wanton destructiveness, classical commentators on violence have emphasized its instrumental function and its peculiar dangers.

The military classic of the Chinese, the *Book of War*, dates from the fifth century B.C., and warns of the limits of violence.

"Now, of the fighting races below heaven; those who gained five victories have been worn out; those who have won four victories have been impoverished; three victories have given dominion; two victories have founded a kingdom; and upon one victory an empire has been established.

"For those who have gained power on earth by many victories are few; and those who have lost it, many."

For modern specialists the political view of war was formulated by Clausewitz when he enunciated the famous theory that "war is a mere continuation of policy by other means." Clausewitz had experience as a Prussian staff officer, and he was impressed by the fact that hostile relations were never a question of purely military effort aiming at the extreme of all that was possible. Available energy was conditioned by expedient calculations of all kinds, especially by the intensity of collective interest in the undertaking at hand. Hence war was rarely, if ever, "absolute war"; it was a detail in a changing context of loyalties, hopes, and expectations.

The dependence of military objectives upon general political circumstances was shown in the American War of Secession. The political object of the Federal States was to prevent Confederate States from leaving the Union. The political object of the South was independence. The North was greatly superior in numbers and in resources, and the South never thought of conquering the North. The general strategy was to prolong resistance, in the twofold hope that the North would be convinced that it was not worth the cost to compel the South to stay in the Union, and that foreign intervention would come to the support of the South.

General Robert E. Lee sought to obtain both of these political objectives by carrying the war to the North, and his strategy from 1862 until the summer of 1863 was offensive. When he was defeated at Gettysburg in July, 1863, he no longer possessed the means to continue an offensive policy, and it became plain that foreign aid was not forthcoming. His strategy was now defensive, with the object of exhausting the power and patience of the North. The North, like the British in relation to the Boers in the South African War, could reach its objective only by defeating the armies of the enemy and by occupying most of the enemy's territory.

Many of the principles of war which are generalized in books on strategy emphasize the connection between the act of violence and its context. The "principle of security" stresses the importance of making sure that the attitudes of those upon whom the operation depends are carefully conserved throughout the enterprise.

Major General Sir F. Maurice shows how the opening campaign of 1862 in the American Civil War failed partly through neglect of this principle of security. McClellan, commander of the Federal forces, had 180,000 men on the frontiers of Virginia. The Confederates had 71,000 men available for the defense of Virginia and their capital, Richmond. The Federal forces had failed the year before in their advance on Richmond, when they had sustained the defeat of Bull Run. During the spring months the few roads were bad. McClellan conceived the plan of utilizing the command of the sea, and transferring the greater part of his army secretly to the Yorktown peninsula, where it would be within sixty miles of Richmond. President Lincoln approved of this plan of campaign on the express condition that adequate provision was to be made for the security of Washington, which is separated from Virginia only by the width of the Potomac River.

General McClellen embarked his troops for the peninsula without taking the President into his confidence, or explaining the measures taken for the protection of Washington. Nor did he ascertain whether General Wadsworth, appointed to command the defenses of Washington, was satisfied that he had enough troops. He simply sent the War Office a list of troops left behind.

President Lincoln ordered a military committee to inquire whether his instructions for the security of the Capital had been complied with. General Wadsworth said that the troops at his disposal were insufficient in numbers and quality, and the President ordered the 1st Corps of McClellan's army, commanded by General McDowell, to remain in northern Virginia and cover Washington. McClellan's attitude had created suspicion in the mind of the President, and lack of confidence soon gave way to alarm when on May 25 General Stonewall Jackson with 16,000 men defeated the defender Banks in the Shenandoah Valley. Panic in Washington led to the diversion of further troops from McClellan and to a wild-goose chase after Jackson.

McClellan and his friends believed that the President was guilty of a breach of faith and of excessive timidity. But the President felt the great weight of his responsibility for the protection of the citadel of the national government, and was quite justified in doubting the reliability of the reticent and seemingly evasive general. McClellan had failed to consider the operation in its entirety; he had neglected to solidify certain attitudes of cooperative confidence indispensable to the execution of the plan.

The effective use of violence implies a preponderance of destructive power at vital places through the entire operation. Many of the principles of war remind generals and rulers of the importance of considering the entire course of the undertaking, selecting points of specific application with a view to all pertinent contingencies. Hence the emphasis upon "economy," "cooperation," "offensive," "movement," "surprise," and "concentration" as means to the general end. Hence, also, the importance of gauging the probability that outside intervention will produce defeat or remove the fruits of victory. In retrospect it is plain that the German high command failed to see the full potentialities of the United States in relation to the European war. Great Britain, on the other hand, adopted contraband rules and practices which were designed to soften American anger.

In the quest for preponderance, the dream of every alert strategist is the development of an offensive so surprising and so destructive that the enemy is rendered incapable of effective resistance. This is aptly called the dream of Cannae. The original Cannae was fought between Romans and Carthaginians at Apulia in 216 B.C. The small army of Hannibal cut 85,000 Roman legionaries to pieces, catching the enemy from the flank with cavalry and surrounding him. Not crude

potential superiority, but specific, actual preponderance is the goal of effective strategy. The famous
Schlieffen plan, which despite emasculation nearly
guided Germany to victory in 1914, was based on this
conception. Schlieffen allotted two-thirds of the entire
German army (fifty-three divisions out of seventy-
two) to one single part of the front, the right wing,
which was to march across Belgium and northern
France on Paris. He sought to augment the fighting
strength of the right by the latest instruments of war,
heavy howitzers and machine guns, which the army
undertook to accumulate in secret in order to obtain
the effect of Hannibal's special cavalry. After crushing
the principal enemy, France, the idea was to turn
against Russia in the east. But the absence of two
corps which were shifted by von Moltke from the
right wing as it was marching triumphantly through
Belgium and northern France was sufficient to block
the realization of victory. The two corps were dis-
patched to the eastern front to ease the pressure on
East Prussia, home of the influential Junkers.

Today the new devices of warfare, airplanes and
gas, inflame the imaginations of ambitious specialists
in violence. Can superior quantities of planes and gas,
secretly accumulated in advance, be sent against the
strongest enemy, reducing him to submission in a few
days or hours, enabling the victor to turn against
weaker enemies, or possibly to crush rebellion at
home? As a rule the lure of technological supremacy
has paved the way to disappointment. It has led to
absorption in mechanical detail, and to the neglect of
the more delicate psychological and social aspects
of the total situation.

Successful violence depends upon coordinating sucn
other salient aspects of the total act as organization.
propaganda, information. Since the demand to secede
usually appears in parts of the state inhabited by
elements which are differentiated from the state as a

whole, it is often feasible to defer large-scale violence until a government within a government has been successfully organized.

Such a government within a government was, and is, the Interior Macedonian Revolutionary Organization, the IMRO, which was founded in 1893 by a group of young Macedonian schoolteachers. It aimed by means of popular agitation to force Turkey to recognize Macedonian autonomy in line with the guarantees of Article XXIII of the Treaty of Berlin. It was open to all Macedonians, whether Serbian, Greek, Rumanian, Turkish, Jewish, or Bulgarian. In 1903 the IMRO fostered an uprising which, though crushed by the Turks, precipitated European intervention. It was not until 1906 that a constitution was ratified by a general assembly of the IMRO. "Macedonia for Macedonians" and "Evolution not Revolution" were the principal slogans. Local committees were elected by universal suffrage; each committee sent delegates to a rayon committee; above this was the okrug committee, corresponding to the vilayet. The okrug committee sent 47 delegates to the regular general congress, which elected the central committee of three. Another body appointed by the central committee represented the organization in the purchase of arms and ammunition from outsiders. No single person was ever given authority. Owing to the breakdown of Turkish administration, the IMRO took over the courts, suppressed brigandage, and maintained schools. Military groups executed the decrees of courts, and a secret village militia stood ready for emergencies.

The case of the IMRO is exceptional. The organization of economics and diplomacy is usually far less complete, especially in revolutionary movements. It is seldom possible in advance of violence to regiment those who are friendly to the objective sought. As a rule, therefore, successful violence is relatively more dependent upon proper coordination with propaganda. Successful violence in revolution depends upon the conjunction of a *coup d'état* with a crisis of mass discontent. The *coup d'état* can be executed by a small number of storm troops which are well informed, armed, and trained; but the chances of securing a loyal conspirative personnel, and of carrying through the action with mass support, depend upon long propaganda preparation in advance of crisis.

This propaganda preparation must be especially designed to win over or to demoralize a large fraction of the soldiery and the police. By the nature of the case, revolutionary forces are certain to be inadequately armed. Thus the 2,000 storm troops which engaged in one of the Canton uprisings had only 200 bombs and 27 revolvers. At Shanghai 6,000 men had weapons for only 150. The proletarian hundreds of Germany in 1923 numbered a quarter of a million, though only a few hundred were armed. Since it is imperative to capture arms early in the uprising, penetration of the armed forces of the established order is crucially important. Proper propaganda preparation ensured a pro-Bolshevik garrison in Petrograd in 1917.

Since the rank and file in any revolutionary rising is composed of comparatively inexperienced fighters who are laboring under enhanced emotional stress, the uprising must be planned to yield conspicuous successes at once. In the Hamburg rising of 1923 careful planning enabled the storm troopers to overpower the men at several police stations and to secure arms. And a little later the workers were clever enough to cut off some of the dreaded tanks by building ditches and barricades behind them.

The cooperation of the masses requires careful timing of the uprising to fit the psychological moment. At Reval the leaders failed to instigate mass protests, even when Tromp, head of the trades unions, was shot, which occurred three days before the rising.

Hence the masses were uncertain what was afoot and hesitated instead of striking. The success of the Bolshevik coup in Petrograd was partly assured by the building up of an atmosphere of general expectancy. Posters and papers constantly asked how the masses were to seize power. The final uprising itself was timed to coincide with the meeting of the Second All-Russian Congress in Petrograd which could then act quickly as a provisional government. It was not even necessary to launch a general strike.

An act of violence becomes "propaganda of the deed" when it is expected that the effect on attitudes will be highly disproportionate to the immediate objective consequences of the act. An assassination is such an instance. The horror with which constituted authority contemplates its own assassination has reduced the amount of calm analysis of this method of obtaining results. Seldom is assassination treated with the detachment exhibited in a famous letter received by Lord Kimberley, Viceroy of Dublin, which began:

"My Lord, tomorrow we intend to kill you at the corner of Kildare Street; but we would like you to know that there is nothing personal in it."

An eligible target for "propaganda of the deed" is some personality whose loss will terrorize the enemy and weaken the unity of will of those who uphold an established order. Or a despotic official may be given a temporary lease on life in order to enable him to serve the cause of secession or revolution by continuing to provoke resentment against the established regime. Sometimes an act of assassination is intended to show that resistance is possible, to destroy legends of invincibility, and to incite mass upheavals.

But it now appears reasonable to conclude that selective assassination fails of its purpose as revolutionary propaganda. The People's Will which was formed in Russia in 1879 relied upon terrorism in the hope of inciting the masses. The actual terrorists were usually from families of the depressed gentry who were inclined to individual romanticism as a means of social protest. The peasants did not rise; hence terroristic tactics passed into disrepute.

An important qualification must be made, however, upon the judgment adverse to assassination as a means of propaganda. Nationalistic aspirations have been furthered by demonstrated willingness to assassinate and to sacrifice. Foreign antagonism to the ruling elite may be brought to a focus by such dramatic acts. Foreign elites may seize the occasion for intervention. This, at least, was accomplished when the IMRO rose against Turkey in 1903, often assassinating government officials.

Plainly it is often advisable for attackers and defenders of an established order to use assassination as a means of ridding themselves of dangerous persons; but other than propaganda considerations are involved in such cases.

In terror, as in assassination, propaganda goals are uppermost, and the overt acts are timed to produce the greatest possible psychological effect. Terror must be ruthless and swift. The destruction of some enemies without delay may paralyze the opposition and save many lives later on. Secrecy is essential; hence the arrests at night, and the disclosure of no information to relatives and friends for weeks or months. The terror was effectively used by the Soviet authorities after the attempt on the life of Lenin in 1918, and after the assassination of Kirov in 1934.

The importance of coordinating violence with information; no less than with organization, is universally accepted. During the World War there were many brilliant examples of how good intelligence about the armed forces of the enemy won battles or avoided losses. A spy in the Russian railway service kept the German staff in East Prussia acquainted with the Russian field cipher during the first two months of the war, enabling von Hindenburg and Ludendorff to take full advantage of the poor coordination between Generals Rennenkampf and Samsonoff, and to win the Masurian Lakes campaign.

Failure of adequate intelligence led to the withdrawal of the Anglo-French Mediterranean fleet under the British admiral, De Robeck, from the bombardment of the Dardanelles. The Turks, sure that Constantinople was doomed, had a train loaded with government archives ready to leave when the astounding news came that the Allied fleet had suddenly sailed away.

In 1917 when the morale of the French troops had been gravely undermined by the apparently insensate demands that had been made upon them for incessant offensive action, mutiny broke out in a certain sector. For the greater part of a day a pivotal point on the front line was held by a handful of artillerymen and sappers; but the Germans did not discover the situation in time to take advantage of the gateway.

Often good intelligence has been ignored by the high command. Witness the incredulity with which the reports were received that the Allies were preparing an offensive with tanks. After the sensational debut at Cambrai, the German experts saw how close they had come to a devastating reverse, had the attack been launched on a larger scale.

Counterespionage seeks to uncover enemy spies, and often scored sensational successes in that war. British agents found that German espionage in Great Britain was organized so that all messages were sent along one channel. By shadowing the lesser agents, the entire German staff was discovered, and they were promptly incarcerated at the outbreak of hostilities in 1914. So complete was this interference with enemy intelligence that as late as August 23 General von Kluck advanced on Mons in ignorance that the entire British Expeditionary Force of 100,000 men was in front of him.

Final action in a revolutionary uprising must be

based on a plan which rests on proper information about the vital positions to take. This requires careful survey of the distribution of armed forces in a given city, discovery of the arsenals and ammunition dumps; location of staff, guards, and lookouts; study of telegraphic, telephonic, radio, and other communication agencies of the high command, and the best ways to control or wreck them; knowledge of the tension between officers and men, and of their attitudes toward the revolutionary program.

The same detailed information should be available about the police forces, and about essential city services, like communication, transportation, water, light, electricity, gas, bridges and streams, principal thoroughfares and squares, addresses of editors and publishers of hostile papers; addresses of government heads, private industrial heads, bankers, and influential persons; location of prisons and the possibilities of freeing prisoners.

Superior local knowledge is one of the assets of the rank and file in revolutionary uprisings. When a genuinely revolutionary situation is chosen, mass uprisings have the advantage of desperate resolve and high morale. Knowing the local terrain, the rank and file can make effective use of it for hiding, sniping, sudden forays, quick escapes. The local police have the same intimate knowledge, but they can be put out of action by sudden attack. The infantry has less familiarity with the terrain in street fighting and is usually accustomed to move in larger units and in more orderly fashion than is most effective. Indeed, small squads may be isolated from their officers and won over to the revolution.

Since the execution of dangerous projects in war or revolution relies so heavily upon the motives and skill of personnel, the choice and handling of men are of the utmost importance. Loyalty to the ideology or mythology of the elite is the prime consideration.

Hence the Soviet army trains those who come from the families of workers or the lesser peasantry; only auxiliary services are open to the sons of former officials, teachers, physicians, merchants, or manufacturers. The German army depends mainly on the sturdy and loyal peasantry, especially for military duty in connection with industrial and urban disturbances. In order to prevent fraternizing between soldiers and the local population, the Russian imperial army depended upon Cossack cavalry in critical situations, and the Dual Monarchy took care to mix nationalities and to depend on a peasant rather than a proletarian rank and file.

Revolutionists have learned to rely on a small band of seasoned professional revolutionaries in preference to a fickle swarm of dilettantes. This was one of the principal contributions of Lenin to the practice of revolution.

Since the use of violence keeps the individual confronted by the possibility of death, it is somewhat incongruous to pay him in cash. Hence the effort to exalt psychological rather than material rewards. Hence the stress on "honor," and the investing of citations and orders with as much mystical potency as possible. This diminishes the cost of maintaining a given volume of effort, and prevents too much reflection about the proportion between risk and return. Seeking to cultivate the spirit of honor, the Soviet army regulations provide for thirteen levels of distinction. Modern armies have come to rely upon honor, and upon systematic indoctrination as a supplement to drills and penalties.

Plainly the astute use of violence depends upon the constant translation of social change into terms of fighting effectiveness. The appearance of gas as a weapon has recently modified the balance of power between the beneficiaries and the challengers of an established order. Authorities have hesitated to use artillery to destroy men, women, and children in entire districts, since attempts of this kind may provoke indignant support of revolutionary action. Hence artillery units have been confined, for the most part, to destroying barricades thrown up in street fighting. Cavalry, of course, is practically unusable in narrow street fighting, since it affords a conspicuous target to snipers. Cavalry can be used in charges against unarmed masses in open squares, but otherwise it is serviceable only for communication. Tanks and armed cars are sufficiently mobile for use in street fighting, and they are not vulnerable to rifle and machine-gun fire. Sometimes, however, they can be stopped by bombs and cut off by barricades. Airplanes can be used to reconnoiter. Their bomb and machine-gun fire can clean out nests of rebels, and their noise is unnerving to the undisciplined populace.

But it is the development of gas that has put in the hands of authority a means of demolishing segregated opposition without holocaust. Rebels can be put out of action without killing the inhabitants of a whole district. It is safe to say that unless an adequate supply of gas can be accumulated in advance or captured at once, street fighting against constituted authority has become futile. But this may be but temporary, for cheap means of gas defense may be discovered, and the balance of fighting effectiveness may be back where it was before.

Whether used for war, secession, or revolution, it is plain that violence must be subordinated to the total operation of which it is a part. Sheer joy in sadistic excess must be chastened by expediency. In a world of limited possibilities, violence is rarely "absolute." Violence is a means to ends to be attained in the developing situation. The attitudes of those upon whom the success of the enterprise depends must be carefully conserved. In the search for predominance of destructive power at vital points, violence must be coordinated with organization, propaganda, information. Special attention must be given to the personal agents of the elite, and to the meaning of any social change for the shifting balance of fighting effectiveness.

FOUR

GOODS

The use of goods in elite attack and defense takes the form of destroying, withholding, apportioning. There may be sabotage or shutdown; strike, boycott, blacklist, noncooperation; rationing, pricing, bribing. Destruction of property is so closely connected with the use of violence on persons that it will receive no special treatment in this chapter, which is limited to withholding and apportioning.

Plainly an elite is subject to domestic attack when it fails to coincide with prosperity. Mounting insecurities may be discharged nonrationally against the symbols and practices of the established order. The result may be no more extensive than the substitution of Tom for Bill in a Democratic parish in Louisiana, or of the Republicans for the Democrats in a border state like Kentucky. But it may involve a revolutionary change in government, as in Germany (1918), or a revolutionary change in social organization, as in Russia (1917). In modern society the oscillations of economic life have become so flagrant that the security of elites is peculiarly bound up with shifts in goods and prices. Hence we are compelled to concentrate upon the strategy and tactics of "economic" relationships.

There are two principal means of directing the flow of goods and services, and elite security is often sought by combining them. We may distinguish systems of *rationing* from systems of *pricing*. Rationing is an act of assigning specific goods or services for consumption or for use in production. Pricing is an act of assigning nonspecific claims to goods and services.

Modern armed forces rely extensively on rationing. Specialists in violence may be rationed the use of specific fortresses, garrisons, age classes of the population, training fields, factories, railroads, motor transports, airplanes. Soldiers are rationed uniforms, guns, food; their schedule of activity is prescribed.

Besides rationed resources, the high command may have many nonspecific claims (dollars, pounds, marks, francs) put at their disposal. A given unit of purchasing power is a nonspecific claim, since it may be spent to buy man power or material equipment.

Rationing systems have often proved highly efficient in the use of resources. Especially during emergencies is it customary for the ruling elite to rely upon this method of controlling the acts and attitudes of the population. The civilian population may receive food cards which call for specified amounts of specific articles. Often, of course, the rationing may be directed primarily toward the control of collective attitudes, and have little to do with its ostensible purpose. During the World War, for example, volunteer sugar rationing was encouraged in the United States. To some extent the purpose was to save the shipping which would have been used to import raw sugar from Cuba and the Philippines, and to increase the amount of sugar and shipping available to the Allies. But perhaps the dominant objective was to bring a sense of the immediate importance of the war effort into the daily lives of American housewives, and hence to the nation as a whole.

The conspicuous disadvantage of rationing systems is that discontent may be massed against the members of the hierarchy who are visibly responsible for the system. Slow, clumsy, or ill-advised action may go so far as to undermine respect for constituted authority. It has been remarked that the recipes issued by the German food administration during the war so often gave ludicrous results that the faith of many simple souls in the infallibility of the agents of the state was undermined.

It is true that pricing methods may suffer from many of the shortcomings of rationing systems. When the price of labor and of commodities is set by conspicuous members of the hierarchy, responsibility is focused upon them. And price fixing may deprive the individual of alternatives just as effectively as a rationing arrangement. If wages and salaries are set sufficiently low by the price fixers, or if the prices on goods are put sufficiently high, money is first spent for such essential items as food, and there may be little left over. It is also possible by the use of direct or indirect taxes to limit the alternatives open to the individual. Contributions or bond subscriptions may be made to appear so necessary that the individual is severely circumscribed.

However, the pricing system may work to veil the responsibility for the apportionment of goods from the eyes of the community. This reduces the probability that some official of a public or private hierarchy will be taken as the target of common discontent. When prices are set in the course of bargains among many equal participants in a market, the price appears to be beyond the control of any determinate person. The apportionment of goods seems to be the outcome of a depersonalized procedure for which no one is responsible.

When the routines of the freely competitive market

are running smoothly, an "invisible hand" would appear to guide the result, and the hand is the hand of one unknown to flesh and blood, incapable of being found and thanked or found and hacked to bits. All pervasive "laws of supply and demand," promulgated by no executive and passed by no legislature, seem to have laid down the slots along which human efforts run their predestined course.

The competitive market among bargaining equals has notoriously failed to stay put. Hence the apportionment of goods through this "impersonal" agency has failed to function to the general satisfaction of many communities. Sometimes those who control the supply (like the local telephone company) seem to get the upper hand; sometimes those who control demand (like the milling companies) seem to dictate the terms of the transaction. The growth of great private hierarchies of big business and big finance have come to the center of attention in capitalistic countries. Discontent, therefore, tends to discharge against them. For a time private hierarchies seek to "pass the buck" to the government, and save themselves by attacking the public hierarchy.

But blackguarding the government is a dangerous game for private business, the most influential elite in modern capitalistic nations. Blackguarding the government undermines respect for duly constituted authority, breaking up the habit of acquiescence in the established system.

The most drastic solution of the conflict between public and private hierarchies occurred in Russia with the abolition of the private hierarchies. Effective decision-making rests in the hands of the political committee of the Communist party. Contradictory viewpoints, however, persist; trades-union members want better conditions for factory workers in relation to agriculturists; some demand more capital goods production, while others insist upon more consumption goods production. Plainly the governmentalizing of social life does not abolish the contradictions which are generated by differentials in relation to production.

But the technique of administration in the Soviet Union has shown how pricing systems can supplement and even supplant rationing systems in a governmentalized society. Goods are distributed by a complex combination of rationing and pricing. Through rationing it is possible to withhold limited supplies from "undesirable" elements, and to starve them out of existence or into submission. Through pricing it is possible to disguise the rationing elements in the system. Thus prices may be set for eggs; but no eggs may be on hand if it is suddenly decided to procure foreign valuta by dumping eggs on the foreign market. Owing to the many complex combinations of pricing and rationing, it has been possible to find several different prices side by side for the same commodity. Only careful inquiry into the rationing aspects of each separate situation enables one to account for the astonishing difference in price level. The price at the factory supply store may be less than in the "open" market; but there may be restricted (rationed) access to the factory store. Contrasting price levels can be preserved in outlets which are accessible to foreign engineers, native engineers, higher officials and party members, lesser officials and party members, skilled workers, semiskilled and unskilled workers, peasants, workers in plants or on farms which made their quota, workers in plants or on farms which failed to make their quota, and so on through a long list of distinctions.

During times of crisis scarcity, the possibility of effective concerted protest can be guarded against by such mixed systems of distribution. The presence or absence of goods becomes an all-absorbing topic of conversation and of fantasy. The clothing card may entitle the "bearer" to a pair of shoes; but will there be shoes at the commissary? The food card may entitle one to "butter"; but there has been no "butter" for two weeks, and perhaps the "oleo" gave out two days ago. Better hoard rubles or marks or lire and take chances with the profiteers in the illegal market?

Like worried, fretful animals, an entire population can be reduced to droves of anxious beasts, concerned with crusts, overresponsive to pats and kicks alike. During periods of "depression" in capitalistic countries the relief population can be reduced in self-reliance and in capacity for collective self-assertion by the demoralizing effect of uncertainty and the multiplication of time-consuming red tape, petty favors, and petty penalties.

It is plain that pricing and rationing are methods available to any elite, whether in Soviet Russia or in the United States. And it is plain that pricing is the safest device of "smooth-water" sailing, but that it requires a supplement of rationing when the breakers of discontent are at hand.

It has been amply emphasized that one of the besetting plights of capitalistic systems is the tendency of competition to pass into monopoly, and to break down the defense of "impersonality" which has stood the system in such good stead. Monopolies also give way to competitive units, but the net historical movement has been toward hierarchies, whether public or private. This has meant that more and more prices are "administratively controlled" [Gardiner Means], whether the administrative hierarchy is public or private. They are not arrived at by bargaining among "equals" in a market.

One way to think of the problem of preserving capitalistic societies is to diagnose the consequences of this development. During depressions the administratively controlled prices can often be sustained at a high level, while competitively determined prices sag. In the United States the prices of manufactured goods are subject to more administrative control at the beginning of a depression than are agricultural prices. Thus the prices of electrical goods like telephones remain stable, while farm products often sell at low levels. As the money income of the farmer declines, he increases his production in order to realize whatever he can so that he may pay taxes, interest, and other obligations dischargeable in money. This tendency toward flooding the market brings down the prices of farm commodities yet further, and limits the ability of the farmer to buy manufactured goods.

Is it possible to work out a concert of vested and sentimental interests which will support the peaceful readjustment of overrigid and overflexible prices?

The great instability of economic life under capitalism has recently been traced to the free creation of circulating media by private commercial banks. Commercial banks have learned how to operate by keeping on hand but a small proportion of cash reserve against liabilities. A loan of $100,000 by a bank is typically made by creating a deposit to the credit of the borrower. This deposit increases the liabilities of the bank; but the loan also increases the assets (accounts receivable) by $100,000 plus interest. On the assumption that the deposit will not be called for at once, the bank is able to lend most of these 100,000 units again, thus creating another deposit and another asset.

The effect of this mode of multiplying circulating media is to build up a vast system of dispersed and pyramided claims which are based upon the tacit assumption that withdrawals will not be made simultaneously. That is, it is assumed that only a small proportion of the participants in the economic process will want cash at any one time. The whole superstructure of interrelationships will collapse when everyone takes the basic assumption of liquidity with sufficient seriousness to demonstrate that when everyone acts upon it, the assumption no longer applies.

These developments of industrial and financial capitalism have produced consequences for which the early expositors of the system were evidently unprepared. Thus it was taken for granted that "saving" and "consumption" were two separate processes which did not go on side by side, but one after the other. This looks plausible to the individual who receives $2,000 a year, and knows that if he saves $500, he cuts down his consumption by $500. Harold G. Moulton, however, contends that it is unsound to project this mode of thought upon collective processes. Using the term "capital" to cover "implements, tools, machines, industrial buildings, railroad tracks, power houses, and other concrete material instruments which aid man in the processes of production," he shows that periods of rapid capital formation, and periods of rapid increase in consumption, march side by side, not single file. This means that the flow of funds to the investment market does not automatically increase the creation of capital equipment. Moulton's analysis shows that savings which entered the investment markets during the prosperous years of the twenties inflated the price of securities rather than promoted a proportionate growth of plant and equipment. And it was the free creation of credit by the commercial banks that made most of this possible.

Hence it is proposed to remodel the routines of capitalistic economy by abolishing commercial banks and separating the deposit from the investment function. This might be done by requiring 100 per cent reserve against demand or short-term deposits. Investing would then represent "real saving." It is anticipated that the most important source of instability would be eliminated. It is not yet plain what combination of vested and sentimental interests, aligned behind this suggestion, would refrain from nullifying policies, such as the direct inflation of the circulating medium by the government. But this suggestion has begun to become practical politics in the United States in the recent depression.

A closely related aspect of modern economic instability and mobility is the weakening of individual ties to particular situations. When we say that a feudal family owns real property, this relationship is most inadequately described by the word "owned." The specific acres, villagers, servants, houses, barns, and driveways are all rich in traditional meaning. Such extreme attachment to specific properties has been attenuated by modern industrial and financial developments. A man who runs a huge wheat farm today may sell out tomorrow and enter the warehouse, milling, or commission business. He is likely to have no interest in passing on specific acres to his heirs.

The search for profits has led to the discovery of ways of making quick transfers from one claim to another. Hence there has been constant increase in the liquidity of claims.

A quantitative estimate can be made of the total volume of liquid assets by ascertaining the debts or claims which are assumed to be convertible within a relatively short time. Stocks and bonds which are listed on exchanges may be included in the computation, since ordinary trading operations are supposed to constitute a mechanism for converting these claims into cash on short notice. Bank deposits should be included, since they are debts of the bank to the depositor, which are presumed to be withdrawable on demand or within a short time. The cash surrender value of life insurance policies has usually been regarded as available to policyholders through a process of lending on a few days' notice.

Plainly these various arrangements for maintaining liquidity function smoothly when the volume of realizations is kept within limits. Wherever attempts are made to collect all bank deposits at one time, to sell all bonds and stocks at one time, to borrow on all life insurance policies at one time, or to force collection of all debts or claims at one time, the whole structure ceases to function. Such stoppages of function are precisely what happens in "panics"; and the severity of these malfunctionings is in proportion to the complexity of the superstructure.

Berle and Pederson have analyzed the ratio of liquid claims to national wealth in the United States. The figure was 16 per cent in 1880, 15 per cent in 1890, 18 per cent in 1900, 20 per cent in 1912. The war decade brought up the ratio to 25 per cent, and by 1930 the figure was 40 per cent. By 1933, third year of the depression, the ratio was 33 per cent.

This vast change in the relationship of person to goods was undermining the attachment of the individual to specific claims to property, and diminishing the connection between claims (ownership) and management. In the early days of private enterprise there was a strong link between ownership and management; this has rapidly weakened. The ownership claims are more often purely formal, depersonalized claims for continued units of nonspecific income. The guarantee of income is the crucial consideration; an opportunity for management is less important. Hence the speed with which demands for guaranteed income spread during adverse years. Hence the profound psychological insecurities generated by the depersonalization of business.

The oscillating behavior of capitalistic economic life is self-destructive precisely in the sense in which any adversity breeds disillusionment with the established order. It would, however, be a mistake to exaggerate the self-destructive tendencies of capitalism. Even oscillation is self-mitigating as well as self-destructive. During prosperity the destiny of the individual or of his subgroup seems to stay in his own hands. Basic uncertainty gives business something of the fascination of a game and a crime: a game, because success depends on combinations of luck and ability; a crime, because success depends in part on deception. From one point of view capitalistic society is a great confidence game, for it feeds on fantastic hopes. Millions throb with the prospect of fabulous riches in an economic system which is inherently destined to disappoint most of them.

The "insecurity prices" on the New York Stock Exchange during the boom put paper riches in the hands of millions; yet the whole thing seemed a little unreal. Despite the famous "New Era Boys," there was an atmosphere of the incredible which cushioned the shock of disenchantment. There was no outburst of moral revulsion because all the time there had been a profound suspicion that success was not a matter of morals, but of luck, smartness, and impostorship. It was a "grand racket while it lasted," a "joy ride," a "swell jag." The bargaining Yankee is still admired because he knows how to use his head to outsmart the other fellow, and this easy-going toleration of mutual fraud is a major trait of capitalistic society.

During prosperity, moreover, persons brought up to live abstemiously, to save, and to work are accustomed to luxurious and self-indulgent ways of life. But many of them never escape the early conscience. When the tide turns, adversity yields its satisfactions: one endures depressions to expiate the claims of conscience.

During prosperity, too, the population "succeeds" by ways of doing and thinking which are inconsistent with effective revolutionary action during depressions. In prosperity the individual is confirmed in private planning, in the expectation that rewards will follow self-assertion, and in individualistic pride in personal responsibility. But mass movements depend on the identification of the individual with collective symbols, collective demands, collective hopes. Individualists persevere in individualistic ways of life well into the depression; and thus far capitalism has been able to recover in the major countries. Capitalistic oscillation would seem to generate the psychological safeguards during its expansion which preserve it during collapse.

There is nothing predetermined about self-recovery, however; and the proposals now current for the protection of the system are compelled to rely upon the motivations and skills which can be recruited within the system itself, subject to all the entanglements of the system.

Striking differences in the distribution of wealth and income, prevalent in capitalistic countries, create constant provocations to attack the system which permits them to continue. Hence the undertone of discontent in prosperity and the overtone of protest in adversity. It is possible to separate, for analytic purposes, the problem of stabilizing capitalism from the problem of equalizing incomes. But it is clear that those who get the largest incomes usually assume that their vested interests are to sustain practices whose objective result is to promote instability. This is the inner contradiction in the policies of the plutocracy bred by capitalism. Policies of concession are clearly dictated by long-run considerations; but what are the intervening steps by which a sufficient concentration of vested and sentimental interest may be elicited? To this question we shall return from time to time in the course of this book.

Since the ruling elite usually has the goods at its disposal, the counter-elites which lead the masses must depend more on propaganda than on goods or violence. The potential economic strength or fighting strength of the masses may be concentrated by patient and prolonged propaganda.

To some extent control over goods is indispensable to any revolution. But until the actual seizure of power the control over goods is more important in its symbolic, that is to say, its propaganda, aspect than in its specifically economic aspect.

Withdrawal from cooperation in consumption, production, and other collective activities has been a principal weapon of the disadvantaged. Sometimes the boycott has drawn attention to conditions which aroused action favorable to the disadvantaged. In 1920 the International Trade Union Federation at Amsterdam called for the boycotting of Hungarian goods in protest against the repressive measures of the Hungarian government against labor. The result was to bring into the news of the world the previously suppressed reports of how the "white terror" avenged itself upon those who had been connected with the "red terror." In 1909 some support was won in America for the Chinese by means of a boycott by Chinese of American goods. The protest was directed against the alleged mistreatment of Chinese in America.

On some occasions nationalistic sentiment has been cemented by means of boycotts and strikes. In 1919 the Chinese nationalists organized a boycott against the award of Tsingtao to Japan. As early as 1905 Indians boycotted British goods and began to encourage domestic production. Such widespread movements of noncooperation as those led by Gandhi in recent years could only occur where the practice of noncooperation is deeply embedded in the culture. To this day in India it is a recognized procedure for a man who has suffered wrong from his neighbor to sit down before the latter's door and starve himself to death. The bare threat is usually sufficient because if the victim were to perish, his ghost would presumably haunt the wrongdoer.

At certain times great expectations have been entertained of the effectiveness of the general strike as a means of social revolution. But it seems to be a weapon of limited utility. A general strike has occasionally been successful when launched by labor organizations on behalf of a demand which was popular with some other class in the community. In 1893 the Belgian general strike, which was enthusiastically hailed as a triumph of labor, was for the extension of the suffrage, a demand with which the middle classes were in sympathy. Other general strikes, like that of Sweden in 1909, failed through lack of support from other classes. In fact, the more specifically "proletarian" the demands have been, the more social formations have been marshaled for defensive action against the strike. Hence a general strike must either be a brief demonstration strike, or intensify a major revolutionary crisis, a resort to violence, a seizure of power. Such was the unmistakable meaning of the general strike of 1926 in Great Britain. The striking unions were confronted by the government's cry of "civil war"; and technical students and other volunteers did sufficiently well operating motor trucks and other essential services to prevent extreme disorganization of vital supplies for the community. In 1917 the general strike was a serviceable weapon at the height of the crisis in Moscow, although it was superfluous in Petrograd. In 1920 the Kapp *Putsch* in Berlin, met by a general strike, collapsed. But the Kapp adventurers were without active support in the community at large.

Until an elite has been disintegrated and discredited by colossal ground swells of insecurity, born of defeat and depression, rationalized by spokesmen of new and rising social formations, it is unassailable by withdrawals from cooperation, like strike and boycott.

Plainly the external position of an elite with reference to rival foreign elites is gravely affected by its control over commodities and services. Goods are both a measure of potential fighting strength and a means of fighting effectiveness. One means for the successful prosecution of war is the management of goods to induce dissatisfaction among enemy peoples, to win over allies, to preserve neutrals, and to strengthen internal morale. In a crisis the resources of the entire community are at stake and profit from a unified emergency administration.

The Central Powers were slowly strangled by the

Allied blockade during the World War. Blockade cut down the supply of rubber, tin, cotton, copper, lubricating oils, and fats. The deficit was only partly made up by substitutes. Oils from the distillation of coal were substituted for lubricating oils of petroleum origin, and food and clothes were constantly modified. But progressive scarcity, like creeping paralysis, undermined the physical stamina and the morale of the population.

The extent to which wealthy powers were able to aid their allies is shown in these figures:

Loans by Great Britain	$ 8,770,000,000
Loans by France	2,817,000,000
Loans by United States	9,523,000,000
Loans by Germany	2,047,000,000
Total (others added)	23,660,000,000

The control over goods is nearly as important in the inter-elite rivalries of peace as of war. During the seventeenth and eighteenth centuries the theories and policies connected with mercantilism led to the imposition of discriminatory duties and prohibitions on the products of hostile countries. Peace treaties often included or were accompanied by tariff agreements which provided for the abolishing of prohibitions, for the renunciation of duties, and sometimes for most-favored-nation treatment. Friendly powers were bound to one another by preferential tariffs, notably in the case of the Methuen Treaty of 1703 between England and Portugal.

Jacob Viner has come to the conclusion that during the nineteenth century there was less relation between tariff policy and diplomacy, although tariffs continued to be used as means of pressure. One protracted series of controversies between Italy and France ran from 1888 to 1899. Since the World War the trend toward self-sufficiency has led to the general adoption of export and import licensing and quota or contingent requirements. Discrimination may be practiced in administrative fact even in contravention of legal duty by means of arbitrary valuations for customs purposes, by boycotting goods of foreign origin in government purchases and contracts, by embargoes on imports of animal or vegetable products in the guise of sanitary regulations, by preferred transportation rates for domestic commodities, and by similar devices.

To some extent considerations of fighting effectiveness have regulated the flow of investment into foreign countries. Before the World War, however, British investments abroad were comparatively little affected by such considerations. For 1914 these investments have been valued at 20 billion dollars, or about one-fourth of the national wealth of Great Britain, and constituted the largest bloc of the world's export capital. Where the sense of international insecurity was acute, as in France, calculations of fighting effectiveness influenced the distribution of loans abroad. In 1914 French foreign investments total $8,700,000,000, or 15 per cent of the national wealth. They were more concentrated in government and municipal bonds than British investments, which were more commonly in private undertakings. Melchior Palyi observes that about half of the foreign investment of France was in countries which were allies of France in the World War, or which were expected to be allies. About a third of the total foreign investment of France was lost as a result of repudiation and of other circumstances connected with the World War. English ownership of capital abroad was reduced by about a quarter, chiefly through the repatriation of American securities.

Many of the transactions which attend the movement of capital across national lines confer special influence upon the lending country. Concessions, or special privileges, range from tax exemption, agreements to spend the proceeds of the loan in the lending country, to the turning over of military, diplomatic, and fiscal control to the nationals or the government of the lending country. These devices of penetration have been most common when the borrowing country does not possess the technology of Western European civilization, when its government is unstable, and when foreign obligations are directly assumed by the borrowing government. Economic penetration depends upon a relative surplus of capital for investment. Since prewar Russia, alone among the great powers, was little industrialized, her landed aristocracy favored direct annexation rather than economic penetration, even as the landholders of many Southern states sought to expand the United States toward the southwest before 1861.

The World War, it will be remembered, broke up the world-wide division of labor, and substituted two self-sufficient, or "autarchic," systems: one composed of the Central Powers, one of the Entente. The expansion of the world market had generated conflicts which put profit seeking into the background, and brought considerations of fighting effectiveness to the fore. Hence the quest for invulnerability, each state seeking to attain economic self-sufficiency by controlling its own centers of iron and steel and food production. A divided and weakened Europe reduced to some extent the pressure on less commercialized and industrialized peoples. This favored the expansion of strong states far removed from Europe (like Japan). Instead of an expanding world economy there are now congeries of contracting local economies. Reduced standards of living intensify insecurity; greater insecurity threatens the traditional system, and the elites which profit by it. Prolonged crisis imperils the dualistic system of private and public hierarchies under capitalism. Big business and financial elites find themselves menaced by agitators skilled in the management of the masses, and by militarists stern in respect for glory, not profit.

Threatened from within and from without, the elites of a given community resort to oscillating policies of centralized, then decentralized control of essential goods and services, rationing, then pricing, sometimes to induce, sometimes to coerce, sometimes to divert. Challenging elites, handicapped by the concentration of goods and services in the hands of the established elites, practice withdrawals of cooperation as a means of heightening the will to power of the disaffected.

FIVE

PRACTICES

The ascendancy of any elite partially depends upon the success of the practices it adopts. These procedures comprise all the ways by which elites are recruited and trained, all the forms observed in policy-making and administration. The constitution, written or unwritten, embodies the practices which are deemed most fundamental to the governmental and the social order. Constitutionalism is a special attitude toward the efficacy of written words, "a name," writes Walton H. Hamilton, "given to the trust which men repose in the power of words engrossed on parchment to keep a government in order."

Since practices are changeable details within a changing whole, an established elite can use them to defend itself by catharsis, or by readjustment. Catharsis, the harmless discharge of tension, may be fostered by such humble devices as the act of showing solicitude for the bereaved. The ruler is wise to attend to the disasters of the community, and to signify his prompt and earnest sympathy to the survivors.

Whether quake, flood, hurricane, drought, or pestilence, the resulting insecurities are potentially dangerous to the social order. Hence the canker of resentment must not be permitted to thrive in lonely sadness. Gestures of condolence plus bread are far more potent than bread alone. It is safer to economize on bread than on condolence.

For purposes of defense by catharsis and minor readjustment an established order can rely upon the rearrangement of its own details. During the nineteenth and twentieth centuries, capitalistic nations have avoided revolutionary upset by minor modifications of the institutional order. To some extent the devices of democratization and education diverted attention from the underlying property system. Discontent drained into crusades for universal suffrage, proportional representation, and free public education. The bourgeois revolution did not abolish undemocratic forms of franchise at one blow, but in a protracted series of taps.

Disabilities in legal status were slowly liquidated at vast expense of crusading zeal and energy. The emancipation of negro slaves held by whites, inaugurated in the British colonies in 1833, was not completed until the act of Brazil in 1888. Forms of domestic slavery were tolerated in the African spheres of influence of the great powers, but the traffic in slaves was illegalized in the Brussels convention of 1890. Alone among the Western nations, prewar Russia divided her people into classes having different legal capacity (nobility, clergy, citizens, peasants, besides Asiatics and Jews). The last trace of peasants' disabilities did not disappear in Germany until 1867. By comity and treaty, most modern nations came to accord aliens practically the same civil capacity as citizens.

Disability upon the wife in the marital community began to be removed by legislative reform in America about 1840, and England followed America, beginning about 1870. The personal control of the father over the child has been curtailed, starting first with criminal punishment for cruelty. Freedom of opinion in religion, art, literature, and science was the drift of the times.

The underlying property system was also preserved by the discharge of discontent into controversies over sumptuary legislation. The social program of the bourgeois revolution was not only negative, in the sense that it abolished restrictions on the market, but positive, in the sense that it turned attention to the possibility of molding a bourgeois style of life by means of legislative prohibitions. The mass of the people, struggling for material prosperity, cultivated the "middle-class" virtues of industriousness and domestic regularity, and with the rise of democracy, legislative policy became more aggressive toward such disturbing influences as gambling, drink, and vice.

Since the illegalization of gambling, drinking, and prostitution did not destroy the demand, the chief effect of prohibitory legislation was to withdraw legal protection from certain business enterprises. These were compelled to provide their own means of protecting their investment and enforcing contracts; hence they paid for gangsters and political favors. In the United States, where administration is decentralized, and there has been little direct control by the nation of urban and local life, the resulting administrative laxity frequently generates "reform waves."

Another safety valve for the discharge of discontents against something other than the property system was religious revivalism. English revivalism began with the Wesleys in 1743. The experiences of mass emotion and the practice of assembling, and to some extent of acting, together were of some importance in shaping the labor movement. But attention was diverted from secular symbols of reform and revolution. Waves of revivalism swept over Germany from 1814 to 1836, appealing to the new urban proletariat and galvanizing them into a semblance of collective action. In such years of depression as 1837 and 1853 the United States was the scene of many intense evangelistic campaigns in the cities where the suffering was greatest.

When the criticism of capitalistic individualism became practical politics, concessions took the form of "social legislation." Money had already been spent to provide educational opportunity for the young, but "social legislation" broadened the scope of the state to assume part of the burden of caring for the superannuated, the disabled, and the defective. Many of the consequences of industrialism shocked the sensibilities of influential groups in society, and it was also feared that certain influences were undermining the military effectiveness as well as the industrial efficiency of the masses.

Fear of monopoly led to demands for government ownership and operation, or at least for regulation. Influential business groups soon discovered that they had little to lose from regulatory commissions. In many cases state regulatory commissions were preferred to local or to national bodies. State control commissions reduced the number of authorities to be controlled, and at the same time retained a sufficiently large number of agencies to handicap any effort to use the government for effective socialization. Such commissions were bulwarks of defense against popular petulance and local exactions. The state as the "umpire of competition" could be induced to suffer from myopia.

The lapping waves of discontent continued, however, to erode the breakwaters which were constructed in defense of the established property arrangements. During depressions, battle lines tended to form more and more around slogans and expedients of basic social protest. In many places the reserve concessions of democratic government ran toward exhaustion. A new disillusionment with democracy was expressed in sharper criticisms of parliament, of the "mere legalism" of the old Bill of Rights, and of the "reality" of democracy.

Viewing the transformations of the nineteenth century in retrospect, A. V. Dicey came to the conclusion that criticism of democratic institutions meant that the task of democracy had changed. At first the goal was destruction; all were united in abolishing old restrictions. Now, however, the destructive task of democracy had been accomplished. It had entered upon a constructive phase; but there was little unity in the discovery of positive goals.

Another way to diagnose the situation was to say that the defensive possibilities of democracy for capitalism were becoming depleted. The forms of democratic parliamentarism were being devalued for the masses, who were more insistent upon the use of democracy for socialized purposes. Democratic practices, therefore, could no longer protect a beleaguered capitalism during recurring crises of discontent. Hence capitalism, it was predicted, would soon abandon democracy and rely upon dictatorship.

Every new revolutionary pattern has a vast repertory of minor changes which can be made in order to cope with the insecurities of the population. This was true of the bourgeois revolution, and it is equally true of the revolution in Russia. In the cataclysm of 1917 the fundamental property relationships were altered, and two major social formations—the landed aristocracy and the private plutocracy—were totally liquidated. Organized life is now governmentalized, and the devices at hand for coping with potential discontent are countless. A unified hierarchy of this kind, as long as it retains competent central direction, can deflect hostilities away from itself by changing from rationing to pricing and back again, if need be. It can appear to the community in protean forms, organizing, consolidating, exterminating, rechristening at will. Differences in money income, once so great under private capitalism, can be rearranged in thousands of minor gradations to stimulate the maximum of individual and small group effort. Many forms of honorific distinction can be invented, and discarded when stigma becomes attached to them.

Plainly it is not profitable to consider any practice apart from the principal features of the context in which it operates. Elite preservation is furthered by judicious combinations of efficiency and acceptability. It is dangerous to sacrifice acceptability for efficiency; and it is dangerous to allow momentary considerations of acceptability to obscure the long-run dangers of some forms of inefficiency.

Judgments about all the traditional patterns of policymaking and administration require constant revision in the light of the purposes to be served in changing circumstances. The perils of overemphasis are only matched by the perils of underemphasis, whether the pattern in question is dictatorship or democracy, centralization or decentralization, concentration or dispersion, functional universalization or limitation, obedience or originality, bias or objectivity.

Crisis demands dictatorship, centralization, concentration, obedience, and bias. Intercrisis permits concessions toward democracy, decentralization, dispersion, originality, and objectivity.

Once reasonably certain of rather general support, a recently established elite can afford to democratize the basis of authority, and to use liberalities and restrictions as chips in the baccarat of catharsis and readjustment. Members of any successful revolutionary party want their friends to join for the sake of security and influence within the party, and there are members of the community who seek the privileges that come from belonging to the new "aristocracy." Hence the party is diluted by members who are insufficiently indoctrinated. These members are disposed to exercise their influence on behalf of conciliatory and temporizing policies. This alarms the "diehard" fundamentalists of a vigorous revolutionary party, and sharpens the contradiction between "orthodox" and "moderates." The men on top of the party pyramid can take advantage of this contradiction to hold first one and then another party element responsible for any recent failures. Hence the celebrated "purges" which expunge "wavering" or "irreconcilable" personalities from the party rolls. Then the process of accretion begins again. Roberto Michels has called the expansion and contraction of revolutionary parties the "accordion rhythm." As a general sense of security increases, the trend is toward democratization.

Although it is necessary to centralize in crises, when prompt, decisive action is safer than malcoordination and delay, centralization has notorious disadvantages. In order to mitigate the bureaucratic consequences of great centralization, authorities in the Soviet Union have encouraged many devices of mass criticism. Wall newspapers are prepared in plants and clubs, and the peasants' correspondence ventilates many grievances and fosters initiative. Plainly, however, mass criticism can be encouraged only when the elite is sufficiently secure.

Modern devices of "attitude measurement" have been applied to the task of keeping the elite informed of the changing waves of discontent. Data are carefully tabulated in "morale charts" to show the spores of disaffection and noncooperation.

The invention of certain technical devices has made it possible to compare the results of administrative effort, and to stimulate honesty and emulation. Sidney and Beatrice Webb have remarked that in the early part of the nineteenth century the business of government in Great Britain, whether national or local government, was honeycombed with "favouritism, corruption, and barefaced peculation." Most of this was swept away by the adoption of the audit, a device which is scarcely a century old. The practice of checking the cash transactions of all public officials by a special class of independent experts has improved the general standard of honesty no less than accuracy, and proved how the "habits of human nature" can be altered on a large scale.

As crisis recedes, governments can decentralize. It is important, however, to manage the decentralization in such a way that central agencies can resume control in lawful ways when future emergencies arise. This is the great technical advantage of the practice of devolution, which invests a subordinate authority with a broad competence, subject to specific reservations and future resumptions. Some of the "home rule charters" in American urban communities exhibit true devolutions of authority. But the scope of this principle in the nation as a whole is circumscribed by the federal practice, which delegates specific and limited authority to a central agency. A necessary concession to acceptability when the federal constitution was drafted, it has often barred the path to efficiency. It is inimical to respect for constitutionality when formal barriers are too high for prompt centralization in crises.

Intimately connected with the expedient degree of centralization is the problem of organizing public authority in legislatures or in assemblies. In nations like the United States, where there has been some degree of exemption from the fear of foreign attack, legislatures have been channels of regional trading rather than national policy. It is abundantly plain, of course, that any national policy implies the consideration of component interests and sentiments. But legislatures create vested and sentimental interests which weight national policy in the direction of patchwork rather than mosaic. The local legislator often devotes himself to the advancement of neighborhood projects by striking bargains on national issues.

Such consequences need not invariably be associated with legislatures. In Great Britain, for example, a singularly delicate set of understandings has been developed which renders it possible to change the effective executive (the Cabinet) only after a general election. Special procedures have been invented to rout local matters through channels which integrate them in terms of national policy. For modern governments, however, it is probably expedient to minimize the effect of interlocality trading by sharing authority with assemblies and not with legislatures.

Thus the Soviet Union operates with an assembly rather than a legislature. The assembly is composed of a great many delegates, meets for a short time, listens to broad reports and discussions of policy, expresses itself, especially by the choice of a continuing committee, and retires. This assembly is an important instrument for procuring acceptance of the policies of the central executive. But it need not be assumed that the tone of the assembly is without influence upon the men at the center.

No doubt there will be many efforts to extend the influence of the assembly and to transform it into an agency exercising the same detailed supervision over policy and administration in the Soviet Union which legislatures have obtained in many foreign lands. But it is doubtful if the authority of the assembly will increase appreciably in the visible future of the Soviet Union, because the specter of external danger is not laid, and in centralization lies preparedness.

There are many ways short of formal centralization by which united action may be attained. The "grant-in-aid" offers tangible inducement to local authorities to conform to centrally defined standards. The device of the executive budget compels the consideration of the total communal enterprise. Both the talk and the practice of planning focus attention upon definite goals, and compel the justification of local demands in terms of inclusive advantages.

Crises not only make it wise to centralize but to concentrate authority. In the acute struggles from 1917 through 1921 in Russia, influence became more concentrated in the Communist party at the expense of rival agencies. Rival parties were at first allowed to persist, but they were presently liquidated as the Communist party established a monopoly of legality. Other influential organizations, like the army, the trades unions, and the cooperatives were all subordinated to the party. That decisive, though piecemeal, liquidation of organized nodules of actual or potential opposition is essential to dictatorship was thoroughly learned by Mussolini and Hitler from the Russian experience. Hitler moved with the utmost dispatch. On May 2, 1933, the old trades-union officials of Germany were ejected from their posts, their buildings and property seized, their members incorporated in a special organization of the National Socialist party. Within a few more days all the political parties were destroyed. Meanwhile hostile elements were "purified" from the government services, and the "totalitarian" state was close to completion.

As crisis recedes in the Soviet Union, the political committee of the Communist party is able, in actual practice, to share more authority with roughly coordinate agencies. Initiative can be permitted in more centers and funneled less narrowly through the principal party conduit. But the committee will doubtless continue to integrate the life of the entire Union whenever a sense of threat, or a chance of expansion, inspires the ruling elite.

Such concentration is difficult in the United States, owing to the system of "checks and balances" which was set up under the influence of certain interpretations of the British constitution and of the laws of mechanics. In moments of extreme emergency when the nation demands action the presidency can eclipse the two coordinate branches of government, the Congress and the court. But when threats recede, the President must rely mainly on the patronage power to preserve discipline on behalf of a national policy, as W. Y. Elliott has recently reminded us. The President cannot force the legislators to contest their seats on matters of grave national concern, which is the alternative always open to the British Cabinet. It is a question to what extent the conflicts between the several branches of the federal government cast discredit upon the capacity of democratic government to act boldly for the collective advantage. Thus respect for constitutionality may suffer once more from its apparent role in the strangulation of action.

Authority can be dispersed along functional lines during intercrisis periods, especially in modern civilized communities, where organized activities play such decisive roles. Functional interests in the United States are quite directly expressed through the hundreds of special agencies which maintain headquarters in Washington or New York and direct lobbying activities toward officials and propaganda activities toward the electorate. This "Third House of Congress" is at least nominally legalized in the institutional plan of the "soviet" or the "corporative" states. In the Soviet Union, Italy, and Germany, crisis has been so continuous that the functional apportionment of authority has proceeded but a little way. The experience of Republican Germany with the Economic Advisory Council plainly showed that on political questions a functional body duplicates the territorial body, or that it is superfluous, since on technical questions sufficient contributions can be made by small administrative advisory committees. If a functionally selected legislature were substituted for the territorial legislature, almost no changes of alignment on political questions would take place.

During crises elites value obedience rather than originality. Suffering all the pangs of inner uncertainty, rulers covet the reassuring tones of respectful coordination. But obedience is often a notorious drag on initiative and efficiency. When regimes are less afraid of losing their position, they are wise to endure some lack of piety in the interest of ingenuity.

It is self-evident that during crises an elite is wise

to recruit administrators and other agents primarily for bias and secondarily for objectivity. Bias in favor of the elite breeds self-confidence among the elite. But bias, like docility, has limitations. Skill in exhibitions of loyalty may become better developed than skill in shooting, accounting, or disciplining. Objectivity is itself a value, since it curbs the impulse to distort reality. Objectivity, or at least the appearance of objectivity, is especially useful in courts and quasi-judicial tribunals.

Objectivity can be fostered by many procedural devices which are intended to diminish the quick passage of impulse into action. Thus evidence presented to a court may be subjected to elaborate rules of inclusion and exclusion. Certain tones of voice and modes of address may be required in courts and legislatures. The function of chairmen may be to safeguard the interests of all who desire expression, and to prevent the discussion group from dissolving into a crowd.

Certain special problems present themselves to revolutionary counter-elites. In general their task is to guide the rebellious impulses of the moment into the ways of action which give permanence and power to protest.

Modern revolutionary strategy takes it for granted that sound procedure calls for the training of a body of professional revolutionaries who are capable of seizing revolutionary opportunities. But it is difficult to state how far it is wise to rely upon mass organizations, or to depend principally upon smaller bodies which specialize in the use of symbols of mass appeal.

In the middle years of the nineteenth century, organizations which enunciated revolutionary goals were agitational-conspirative, and hence small. In the ensuing years, organizations in the name of the proletarian revolution often grew to embrace many millions. Germany and Austria were the scene of Social Democratic movements which rivaled in structural complexity the intricacy of capitalism itself. Such organizations and suborganizations developed elaborate bureaucracies which were usually exempt from physical danger in the performance of their duties. They peacefully edited, orated, organized.

Where socialism spelt danger, as in Russia, the agitational-conspirative methods came to prime expression. This did not mean that tiny conspirative cells bore the brunt of revolutionary struggle and committed acts of individual terror. Very considerable organizations were constructed, but they were limited to those who were seasoned to the dangers of protest. Elsewhere, immense membership structures lacked fighting vigor. The sheer labor involved in the internal management of these complicated organizations bound energy inside the organization in petty drudgery and ceremony. Oligarchical tendencies, described by Roberto Michels, produced a spiritless monstrosity when the hour of opportunity struck. Evidently there had been too much mass organization in proportion to mass appeal.

Operating from the triumphant center of revolution, the Third International undertook to subordinate national initiative to the decisions of the central hierarchy, which remained under Russian influence. Since a major revolutionary movement does not develop as a local but as a general movement of protest, the elite which arises to power is assured of moral support from abroad. The Russian elite was saved by the sympathetic cooperation of masses and mass organizations whose threats of revolution handicapped the hostile efforts of established governments. Thus Great Britain was prevented from giving unrestricted aid to Poland against Russia, and to White generals operating against the Soviets, because British statesmen were constantly hampered by the British workers.

The Third International tried to crystallize all this sympathy in a central organization in which, in fact, the Russian group would preponderate. This subjected the leaders of all foreign proletarian organizations to a damaging cross fire. If they supported "foreign" symbols of class war, they were open to devastating attack by spokesmen of the middle class, plutocracy, and aristocracy as antipatriotic and antinationalistic. But if they failed to subordinate themselves to the Third International, they were open to attack from some of the most dynamic and impatient elements inside the laboring class.

Even formal affiliation with the Third International did not assuage the crisis. Very often the measures demanded by the highly centralized organization in Moscow seemed much better adapted to serve the diplomatic expediencies of the new regime than to advance the cause of socialist revolution. Local communists were open to the jibe that they were the "Foreign Legion of Russia" rather than the vanguard of the socialist revolution.

The inner crises of German communism expressed these contradictory tendencies in the sharpest possible manner. There was a split in 1919 over trades-union policy, parliamentarism and Russian dictatorship. The Levi crisis came in 1921 after the unsuccessful "March days." In 1923 the failures in Saxony and Thuringia led to the expulsion of the Brandler group and the building of a communist opposition. In 1925 the "ultra-left" era of Ruth Fischer and Maslow was liquidated in another split. The history discloses many sharp dissensions over individuals and tactics which did not produce a serious break. Efforts were made to smash the Social Democrats by the formation of rival parties, trades unions, military and youth organizations. Plainly it was not foreseen that before the Social Democracy could be demoralized the defensive measures of the established order would find expression in a movement which would decapitate communists and Social Democrats alike. The overcentralized Third International, dominated by and for what were supposed to be the interests of the revolution as embodied in the Russian government, split the masses for the benefit of Fascism.

The implication is that when truly revolutionary movements have seized power anywhere it is wise to relax control from the center, and to permit foreign revolutionary processes to mature along separate national lines.

For elites and counter-elites alike it is wise to avoid rigid loyalty to specific devices. The ebb and flow of collective insecurity threatens whatever *is* with disgrace; and whatever is next will be discredited in time.

PART III: *Results*

SIX

SKILL

Political analysis is not only interested in the methods by which the influential are protected or superseded. It is also concerned with the characteristics of those who obtain such values as deference, safety, income. One aspect of the matter is the partition of values among the exponents of various skills.

A skill is a teachable and learnable operation, and skills include the technique of manipulating things or the symbols of things (skills of manual workers or engineers), the technique of manipulating ceremonial symbols, and the techniques of violence, of organization, of bargaining, of propaganda, of analysis.

It is plain that craftsmen and all who exercise the semiskills connected with the simpler manual operations seldom rise to eminence. The German Reichstag election of 1919 coincided with acute social crisis and the tide was running "left." Yet the new Reichstag had among its members only 2.4 per cent who were "workers," 2.1 per cent who were "salaried workers," and

1.9 per cent who were "craftsmen." The grand total for the manual skills was thus 6.4 per cent, which was remarkably similar to the situation in the Reichstag of 1912. Then the "workers" accounted for 0.5 per cent of the total membership, "salaried workers" were 1.8 per cent, "craftsmen" were 2.5 per cent, and the grand total was 4.8 per cent.

Agriculturists are almost universally underrepresented in proportion to numbers. Exceptions appear principally where agriculture is run according to a system which transforms the nominal farmer or estate holder into an administrator of persons rather than a manipulator of things. Small farming communities are prone to allow themselves to be represented by lawyers or other specialists in the handling of people by means of symbols.

It is noteworthy that engineering skill, so prominent in our society, has seldom led to the posts of greatest eminence. The heroes of the people have seldom been engineers or physical scientists. This remains true despite all the opportunities which have arisen as a result of the application of mechanical, electrical, and chemical energy to production. Wholly new specializations have arisen, concerned with chemistry, electricity, aeronautics, gas, steam, and radio; and older engineering branches have been profoundly modified. The sensational glut of new devices sometimes obscures the long history of specialization on the handling of nature. One may recall the attainments of Egyptians, Babylonians, and Chinese in grading, crowning, and bridging military roads; in constructing fortifications with walls, towers, gateways, moats; in laying out cities and supplying them with water and sewerage systems. Harbors included lighthouses, dredged channels, breakwaters, wharves, warehouses, cranes, windlasses, and water supply. Great works of land reclamation called for dams, irrigation, and drainage. Temples, cathedrals, monuments, and other public edifices and private dwellings are found in the ruins of early civilizations which flourished in Middle America and elsewhere.

So absorbed have the engineers been in the gratifications of their calling that they have been singularly free of outspoken occupational imperialism. They have rarely been articulate in demanding the control of high policy and administration, and in eliciting the support of the masses in the name of some complimentary mythology. In the United States the most elaborate case for the engineer has been made, not by an engineer, but by the economist Thorstein Veblen. In *The Engineers and the Price System* (New York, 1921) Veblen indicted the predatory captain of industry and proposed a system of economic organization in which production and distribution would be determined by engineers. The term "engineer," however, was so broadly defined that it far transcended the customary meaning of the word. The nearest approach to a popular movement spoke in the name of "technocracy," and reached a brief heyday of fame during the great depression after 1929. "Technocracy" was in many ways a very fortunate coinage; it avoided the doctrinaire implications of an "ism," and capitalized the prestige of the terms "technology" and "democracy."

The engineering indictment of the prevailing system runs in terms of waste, and the way to a utopia of plenty is by scientific management. The studies of waste which have been conducted by the Taylor Society in the United States are harbingers of a future when the engineers may rise to greater skill consciousness.

Those who specialize less in the management of things than in the management of the symbols of things are physical scientists. They suffer from the disabilities of the engineer in reaching for the highest posts of deference. It is true that Painlevé was a mathematician and a successful parliamentarian, that De Valera is a mathematician and an Irish nationalist, and that Weizmann is a chemist and a Zionist; but these are exceptional rather than typical.

The physician is an interesting combination of skills, for he learns much of physical technique, but he cannot wholly neglect interpersonal factors. Although the practice of healing brings the practitioner into intimate contact with people, few physicians have risen to posts of general prominence in modern public life. That Clemenceau was a physician in early life had little to do with his final career. In small communities where any learned profession may be believed to equip the individual to grapple on even terms with the "city slickers," physicians may enjoy deference in collective movements. Even so, it is unusual to find as many doctors as there are in the Irish Dail and the Irish Senate (14 in 213 members). Occasionally a physician to an influential king or dictator has won the confidence of his client and patron. When knowledge was less differentiated than today, persons who are reported to have studied medicine more often rose to diplomatic or administrative distinction. But it is not always possible to make out exactly what they studied under the name of medicine.

On the whole it seems reasonable to adhere to the view that heroes, and influential figures behind the scenes, are usually recruited from those who specialize in the management of men rather than the management of things. The control of conduct is the essential skill even when this is associated with elaborate technical skill in engineering or physical science.

The role of skill in violence among the heroes of mankind scarcely needs to be remarked. However, it is true that fighters have often been devalued for long periods of time. Western European civilization has assigned so much importance to the accumulation of property that the prestige of warriors has dwindled. In China the low regard in which fighting men are held has become proverbial.

But specialists in violence obtain a new lease on

life when internal and external crises arise. It is notorious that every war and revolution leaves a legacy of military personages in its wake. In addition to General George Washington the list of candidates for the presidency of the United States who have had a military record includes Jackson, Harrison, Taylor, Scott, McClellan, Grant, Hayes, Garfield, Hancock, Harrison, McKinley, Theodore Roosevelt.

In some societies the road to eminence is not by fighting but by ceremony, as among the Zuni of the American Southwest. Within any society the most striking examples of those who sustain themselves by means of symbols are those who are devoted to ceremony. As the term is here understood, the true ceremonial act is one which involves a minimum of change in overt communal relationships, and is supposed to benefit the community as a whole. It is a true ceremony, in this sense, to perform a dance which is supposed to safeguard the fertility of the soil and the growth of crops. The dance works a minimum change in overt relationships, and is an act which we call "socially internalized." Such an internalized act may be contrasted with the act of judging between two claimants for property, or the act of joining in a raid on a neighboring community. Such acts modify overt relationships. They are "socially externalized."

In most communities there are persons who derive their influence and their livelihood by specializing in true ceremonies. Some ascetics spend their time in seclusion and prayer, obtaining expressions of deference and gifts of goods from the environment. Some priests spend their time in retreat or in the conduct of ritually prescribed operations which modify the emotional responsiveness of those who know about them, but work no other change in the situation.

In some societies the amount of specialization upon socially internalized acts is very insignificant. Every man may be his own priest and magician, communicating directly with a guiding spirit, and obtaining possession of objects and practices which are believed to have automatic power. Where a bit of stone is preserved because it is supposed to bring good luck, it is magic; when the stone is entreated and cajoled as if it were human, it is religion. As Ruth Benedict expresses the difference, magic is technological and mechanistic, while religion is animistic.

Field workers have estimated that a third of the time of some Pueblo Indians is given over to the rehearsal and performance of acts, principally dances, which are ceremonially important. But the number of those who specialize exclusively in ceremony is unimportant. It is notable, however, that many societies support a priesthood which mediates between the individual and the personalized universe.

Such priesthoods are found in varying degrees of helpfulness or rivalry with chiefs. Sometimes the ceremonial function becomes entangled with a host of additional functions. Chieftainship and priesthood are sometimes merged in a single office. Through consolidation chieftains have risen to wider control, and become emperors, fusing royal and priestly prerogatives. The Emperor of Japan, as Son of Heaven, is the highest priest of the land. The Emperor of Rome was Pontifex Maximus.

Sometimes the emperor has been immobilized through the exaggeration of his ceremonial duties. So it was in feudal China: the chief overlord preserved his peculiar potency by devoting himself entirely to the life of the court and to etiquette. Imprisoned by the court, webbed around by etiquette, the overlord reigned only on condition of remaining passive, of ordering nothing in detail, and of refraining from direct administration. He could act only through the simple efficacy of prestige, exercising less power of command than power of inspiration, more often associated with the chief of a sacred hierarchy than with the chief of a state.

The process by which a priestly elite may retain its

sacerdotal symbols and add externalized functions as well can often be traced from historical data. The priestly elite which assisted in the performance of the priestly duties of the emperor developed into a priestly bureaucracy in China and a priestly caste in India. In Rome the various tribal priests were assimilated into a comprehensive *sodalitas;* but in Greece the tribal priests remained separated, never forming a unified priestly caste. In the new kingdom of Egypt the priestly caste was a serious challenge to the authority of the state. Although important from the earliest times in Babylon, the priests gained the upper hand in Israel only after the Exile. In Western Europe the priests predominated after the collapse of the Empire in the west, and they were curbed only as a result of movements which were usually led by secular authorities on the periphery of their sphere of influence. These authorities cooperated with the lesser clergy who were in revolt against the centralization of control at Rome. Such was the social composition of the most active elements in the Reformation.

Much of the history of Western Europe has pivoted on the rivalry of elites for the control of all the symbols capable of arousing submissive responses from the masses. Sometimes both "sacred" and "secular" symbols have been claimed by those who had previously been regarded as specialists in the one or the other. This was signalized in the struggles of Pope versus Emperor.

The effort to do away with "sacred" symbols of any kind, undertaken in the Soviet Union, is almost unique. The usual course of totalitarianism is to seize control of "sacred" symbols and to exploit them for control purposes. An influential element in the National Socialist party is determined to develop a purely local system of sacred symbols which will detach Germans from loyalty to religious vocabularies and customs beyond the frontiers of Germany. As long as there are Germans who feel themselves "Catholic,"

"Protestant," "Jewish," or even "Christian," just so long is a source of disunion at hand. It is feared that the discontented will invoke support from abroad in the name of these sacred symbols. Hence the plan is to abandon the "Jewish-Christian" God and to return to the god symbols which were current before the "Jewish-Christian God" was "foisted" upon the "Aryans."

In the United States the secular elites have sought to minimize the influence of priests and clergymen in politics by proclaiming that they, themselves, championed Christianity and religion. The implication is that the participation of the clergy in government is unnecessary in order to protect religion, especially since the clergy are associated with the special interests of particular denominations. The secular politician stands as the spokesman of the most inclusive symbols of piety, and is confronted by a disunited front of ecclesiastical rivals.

This review of the ceremonial elite, as typified in the priesthood, has shown how often the specialist on ceremony has become a specialist on organization, enhancing his role in the life of the community. He has sometimes moved over to the control of marriage, family, inheritance, and many other overt social relationships. Skill in organization, however, need not be associated with ceremonialism. Skills in keeping accounts, collecting taxes, recording titles, handling correspondence, recruiting, training, supplying are often independent avenues to wider influence. Skill in coordination becomes more essential as the division of labor grows more complex, or as the scale of concerted action is broadened in scope. Conquering chieftains have seen their triumphs wither into dust in the absence of the organizing skill of a bureaucracy. The "bureaucratic culture pattern," traced with care by W. C. MacLeod, has exercised a standardizing influence over the course of political organization.

Skill in bargaining has been so important in the world of business and diplomacy that it may justifiably be singled out for independent consideration. With the gradual dissolution of customary restrictions on the terms of transactions, modern industrialism has, until recently, widened the scope of the competitive market. Skill in "buying cheap and selling dear" became a royal pathway to wealth and distinction.

Another major skill is advocacy, especially in the form of propaganda. There are forms of propaganda in which the personal convictions of the propagandist are important. This is true in the missionary activities of the proselyting religions, and it is true of the propaganda of revolutionary movements. Where personal danger is involved, conviction counts. But most modern propaganda is carried out under the direction of those who have no particular convictions about what their clients want. The modern public relations counsel or advertising agency or press agent has the same code as the lawyer, without the restraints which surround the lawyer. They accept fees to organize symbols to promote the attitudes desired by their clients. The late Ivy Lee rose to eminence as a counselor of the Pennsylvania Railroad, of the Rockefeller interests, and of other important clients. Shortly before his death he disclosed in a Congressional investigation that he had been retained by the German dye trust to advise on their problem of handling the attitudes of the American public toward the German government. Only after the World War did the propagandists begin to attain public recognition, and to overcome the earlier associations with the theatrical press agent or the loud-mouthed spieler at a side show.

Another important symbol skill is in the analysis of human relations. The extension to the relationships among men of the same objective attitude with which men approached physical nature is not qualitatively new. The classical writings of Kautilya, the East Indian, or Aristotle, the Greek, or Machiavelli, the Italian, testify with sufficient eloquence to the penetrating detachment with which some men have become equipped. But the growth of a sizable body of scholars devoted to history and the social and psychological sciences is quite recent. From the mother matrix of law, philosophy, theology, and history have come economists, political scientists, sociologists, social psychologists, individual psychologists, cultural anthropologists, human geographers, social biologists, and many other skill groups.

The connection between priestly skill and analytic skill has often been most intimate. Some priesthoods have specialized as seers, divining the future and stating the courses of action available in the present, thus rendering themselves of signal importance in policy and administration. Concern for the correct pronunciation of words in sacrificial incantations and cult songs made phoneticians and grammarians of the early Brahmans. With the growth of writing the priest often became historiographer and author of sacred codes, guardian of archives, editor of prayers and songs. As theologian he systematized teachings about the number of gods, and perfected the practice of dialectic.

In Western Europe the secularizing of intellectual skills has gone forward gradually through several centuries. Hanseatic merchants sought to emancipate themselves from the clerics by establishing municipal schools of their own. The growth of bookkeeping in Italian cities furnished an occupation for secular intellectuals. The prestige of Arabic and Greek knowledge during the Renaissance created a personality style for wealthy merchants who were supposed to support gentlemen of letters to flatter and instruct them. The rediscovery of printing from movable type, and the spread of cheap publishing, reduced the clerical monopoly of knowledge. The growth of bureaucratic posts multiplied the number of secular livelihoods available, and strengthened the secular gentry against upper secular and ecclesiastical groups. The breakup of the Roman Catholic Church fostered the fragmentation of Christendom and separated secular and sacerdotal authority more sharply than it had been before. With the spread of free public schools, the control of learning passed further out of the hands of the clergy and into the custody of the servants of the secular state.

There are several forms of intellectual expression which supplement, and which also rival, one another. The skill struggles among the practitioners of the intellectual arts often take the following shapes: *naturalistic* versus *normative, systematic* versus *impressionistic, expository* versus *depictive.*

The naturalistic style of discourse uses words which state conditions rather than preferences. The normative style abounds in terms like "ought," "good," "ugly." The modern social sciences emphasize the naturalistic modes of expression. Ethics, aesthetics, and some aspects of epistemology and metaphysics fall in the normative category. Political science is naturalistic; political philosophy is normative. In practice these distinctions are of relative emphasis rather than total exclusion.

Social conflicts afford ready opportunity for advancement by the use of "ought" words. Symbol specialists are demanded who can invent or elaborate the language of justification for the exercise, or the denial, of authority. Contrasting demands are thus defended by appeals to legality, morality, or religion; and decisions among contending parties are couched in the same vocabulary. Lawyers, trained in the canon, Roman and common law, were conspicuous in the defense of the princes against the papacy, and of the monarchs against the nobility. During the eighteenth century when the tides of social criticism were running high against the monarchical system, the symbol makers were the *philosophers,* who as a rule were less professionalized than lawyers or theologians. In the same way it was nonacademic intellectuals who bore the responsibility of protesting against the advance of capitalistic society. There is some evidence that academic intellectuals were more conspicuous in national-istic than in drastic revolutionary movements.

The prominence of polemical journalists, pamphle-teers, lawyers, and theologians need not distract at-tention from the steady increase in the number of those who are supported in society because they can describe and compare many of the more complex routines of social life. They are constantly in demand for advice and support, whether they rise to popular recognition as members of a "Brain Trust" or no. Most of the current social sciences were once com-prehended within the general term "moral philoso-phy." The first chair of "political economy" in the United States appears to have been occupied at Co-lumbia University in 1818, and similar establishments spread gradually over the country. Political science took shape more slowly, although Dr. Thomas Cooper began to teach chemistry, politics, and political econ-omy at South Carolina College in 1811. As a rule the connection was intimate with philosophy and law, and retained much of the normative tone of those disciplines.

Since the professional demand for lawyers was great, efforts were made from time to time to broaden the curriculum of the law schools. When Francis Lieber was called to Columbia in 1857, it was hoped that he could overcome what was called the narrow specialization of law students by attracting them to courses in history and political science. This was a failure, and Lieber himself was finally transferred to the law school where he taught constitutional history and public law. The School of Political Science which was finally organized at Columbia University in 1880 at the initiative of John W. Burgess was the outcome of another unsuccessful effort to break down law school specialization.

The professors of moral philosophy were often so far out of touch with the new routines of business and government that they were at a loss for timely and relevant illustrations of classical aphorisms in terms of modern life. This discrepancy made it possible for new generations of specialists to gain attention by concentrating upon the task of describing the new routines of the expanding civilization in which they lived. This greatly increased the academic emphasis upon the naturalistic at the expense of the normative.

The processes just sketched in the United States were common to all the areas having contact with European civilization. Plainly a thirst for description and for comparison depends chiefly upon the appearance of novel phenomena. At first the impetus in this direction was "extensive" rather than "intensive." The age of discovery opened the minds of Western Europeans to the existence of cultures which contrasted notably with their own accustomed standards. The new world of the Americas and of the Orient, the rediscovered old world, revealed by the revival of classical learning and the excavations of the new archaeology, were refreshing experiences. Later stimulus was supplied by the "intensive" complication of the modern world through the growth of modern technology. The craving for naturalistic orientation went side by side with the growth of new demands and justifications. But so vast was the field of phenomena that normative preoccupations yielded ground to the naturalistic.

Another line of mutual support and of cleavage in the intellectual world is between systematists and impressionists. Systematizers are constantly moving toward an elaborate and logically consistent structure. Impressionists are content with less rigidity of form. In the former group is the treatise writer; in the latter, the essayist, the popular lecturer, the conversationalist, the editorial writer. In periods of stress, opportunities for distinction are open to those who know how to use a medium to arouse the emotions of the masses. Hence treatise making may be abandoned for pamphleteering or oratory by those who are able to master the impressionistic media.

But any new social order, or any slowly maturing movement of social protest, affords abundant opportunities for the systematizer. The Encyclopedists of the eighteenth century were interested in systematizing the new knowledge as a means of modifying the prevailing social system. Treatises like those of Marx and Engels could contribute to the literature of protest in a literate society where the currents of revolution gathered strength for many years. After a new regime marches to power in modern society, the work of codifying its symbolic defenses goes forward. The Italian Fascists used ephemeral media of communication during the seizure of power; but once in the saddle, began work on the Fascist encyclopedia.

Another distinction is between expository and depictive skills. Exposition tends toward the abstract; depiction moves toward the concrete. Depictive skill includes descriptive prose, poetry, drawing, painting, and related media. Some expositions are entirely devoted to the definition of terms and the formal statement of their interconnection. Such was Pareto's *Cours d'économie politique*. Sometimes the rich detail is summarized in elaborate quantitative form, as in Wesley Mitchell's *Business Cycles*. A more frequent form of exposition is to embellish the abstract definitions and propositions by illustrations. (The procedure in this book, for example.)

The skill struggle among exponents of different styles of discourse is often expressed with the utmost acrimony. The treatises of the systematists are often dismissed as idle pedantry, flights from reality, perversions of intelligence, and conspiracies at obfuscation. The essays of the impressionists, on the other hand, are often dismissed by the systematists as glib, irresponsible word-slinging. Academic environments foster the systematist; hence the acrid odor of the term "academic" in the nostrils of the impressionists.

No less pungent has been the exchange of discourtesies between expositors and depictors. Most of the "art" forms of our civilization are depictive. Spokesmen of the depictive may complain of the insufferable dullness of the expository style, and declare that the word moves with its "heart," not its "head." Expositors may dismiss the depictive as pandering to infantile ways of thought, prophesying that a more rational world will forsake the products of the "picture mind."

Those who excel in naturalistic analysis may proclaim the virtues of "objectivity" and refer with condescension to those who imagine the world is interested in the lengthy elaboration of their system of private preferences. The specialists on normative styles of speech may refer disparagingly to the absence of ethical fervor of the ostriches who bury their heads in the sand of science while the war of values is upon us.

Thus each of the skill specialists has at least the rudiments of a mythology in the name of which extra units of the available values may be elicited from his fellow men. The pattern for mythmaking by intellectuals was set for our society by Plato, who dreamed poetically of the "philosopher king" in whom omniscience was at one with omnipotence. For the symbol specialists as a group, both the intellectuals, in the narrow sense of those who specialize on the contentious, and the physical scientists, one of the most active mythmakers is H. G. Wells. Although he may single out the novelizing aesthete, the backward pedagogue, the otherworldly scholar, the smug university intellectual for opprobrious comment, Mr. Wells exalts the "mental worker."

We learn in the *Experiment in Autobiography* (page 2) of Mr. Wells that the mental worker leads not a subnormal, but a "supernormal" life. His is not an "escape"; it is a "way to power."

Mankind is realizing more and more surely that to escape from individual immediacies into the less personal activities now increasing in human society is not, like games, reverie, intoxication or suicide, a suspension or abandonment of the primary life; on the contrary it is the way to power over the primary life which, though subordinated, remains intact. Essentially it is an imposition upon the primary life of a participation in the greater life of the race as a whole. In studies and studios and laboratories, administrative bureaus and exploring expeditions, a new world is germinated and develops. It is not a repudiation of the old but a vast extension of it, in a racial synthesis into which individual aims will ultimately be absorbed. We originative intellectual workers are reconditioning human life.

Passing time includes the rise and fall of skill combinations of every description. It seems that during the feudal age in Europe skill in fighting was a major avenue to power. Later, skill in organization was essential to the consolidation of the national monarchies. Skill in bargaining brought the private plutocrat into his own during the nineteenth and early twentieth centuries. The insecurities of the world of the twentieth century, manifested in world war and revolution, have fostered the chances of the man of skill in propaganda (witness Lenin, Mussolini, Hitler). Once new ideologies have been consolidated in the sentiments of the community, the role of the propagandist will diminish: for the benefit of the man of violence? the bargainer? the ceremonializer?

SEVEN

CLASS

Political analysis includes the class consequences of events. A class is a major social group of similar function, status, and outlook.

A revolution is a shift in the class composition of elites. The influence of the Southern landed aristocracy on American politics was curtailed as a result of the Civil War. On the world stage there was no significant novelty about substituting commercial and industrial capitalists for landed proprietors. This change had occurred under circumstances of catastrophic violence in France at the end of the eighteenth century. In world perspective, the American Civil War did not, but the French Revolution did, signify that a new social formation had risen to greatest influence. The French Revolution, therefore, may be called a world revolution. After the revolution in France the next world revolution took place in Russia in 1917.

World revolutions have been accompanied by sudden shifts in the ruling vocabulary of the elite. Said the absolutist James I of Great Britain, in the days before the gentry revolution:

"It is atheism and blasphemy to dispute what God can do . . . so it is presumption and high contempt in a subject to dispute what a king can do, or to say that a king cannot do this or that."

In the same strain are the words of Bishop Bossuet, commissioned by Louis XIV with the education of the Dauphin, before the bourgeois revolution:

"As in God are united all perfection and every virtue, so all the power of all the individuals in a community is united in the person of the prince."

When the monarch and the aristocracy were swept away, a wholly new vocabulary was employed by those who sat in the seats of the powerful. Declares article 1 of the Declaration of the Rights of Man and the Citizen, adopted by the French National Assembly on August 26, 1789, "men are born and remain free and equal in their rights." Article 2 enumerates the "natural and imprescriptible rights of man."

When the monarchy, aristocracy, and plutocracy of Russia were supplanted, another potent vocabulary was invoked by those who seized authority. The proclamation issued by Lenin, as chairman of the Council of People's Commissars, November 18, 1917, read in part: "Comrades: Workers, Soldiers, Peasants, All who Toil! The workers' and peasants' revolution has finally been victorious in Petrograd, scattering and capturing the last remnants of the small bands of Cossacks duped by Kerensky. . . . The success of the revolution of workers and peasants is assured, for the majority of the people have already come out in its favor. . . . Behind us are the majority of the toilers and the oppressed of all the world. We are fighting in the cause of justice and our victory is sure."

From the "divine right of kings" to the "rights of man," from the "rights of man" to the "proletarian dictatorship"; these have been the principal vocabulary changes in the political history of the modern world. In each case a language of protest, long a utopian hope, became the language of an established order, an ideology. The ruling elite elicited loyalty, blood, and taxes from the populace with new combinations of vowels and consonants.

These sudden changes in class composition of elites introduced innovations in practice as well as in vocabulary. The French Revolution introduced and presently established universal manhood suffrage, church disestablishment, relative freedom of agitation and discussion, the supremacy of parliament over the executive, and abolition of all manner of legal discriminations among classes. Policies favorable to the growth of commerce and industry were instituted by rearranging the system of tariff and taxation. Individual proprietorship was encouraged by transforming peasants into landholders. All this was legitimized in the name of the rights of man, and cemented in walls of intense nationalistic sentiment.

The pattern of the Russian Revolution of 1917 took shape at different phases of the revolutionary crisis. Conspicuous has been the governmentalization of all forms of organized social life. By the end of June, 1918, banks and insurance companies, large-scale industry, mines, water transportation, and the few railroads which were formerly operated by private companies were nationalized. Foreign debts incurred by the Czarist and the Provisional governments were repudiated, foreign investments in private industry were confiscated, and foreign trade monopolized. Presently was begun the abolition of the peasant as a distinct social formation by the development of great collective farms.

The control of affairs was gradually monopolized by a single political party which assumed a monopoly of legality. When the revolution got under way, there were several potent centers of influence in Russia, of which the Communist party was but one. The Soviets were centers of initiative which were by no means under the united discipline of the party; and there were rival political parties. The trades unions and the cooperative societies were only gradually brought under the iron rule of the party during the grinding years of bitter struggle against the perils of intervention, famine, and revolt. Crisis forced concentration or collapse, and the political committee of the Communist party became the directive center of the state.

Within the framework of the governmentalized society, differences in money income were less striking than they had been in the prerevolutionary society; this comparative equality was particularly conspicuous during the period of incessant conflict before 1921. The road to individual success now lay chiefly through the Communist party, which gave access to the principal posts of influence.

This was a "dictatorship of the proletariat," or at least a dictatorship in the name of the proletariat. It was not a socialist state, because democratic forms were not yet permitted. It was not a socialist society, because the government was still constrained to use coercion; "the withering away of the state" was an aspiration for the future, whenever a voluntary consensus among functional groups in the new society should emerge.

World revolutions are valuable landmarks in the understanding of intervening events. Thus some events after the French Revolution can be considered to facilitate, and some to retard, the spread of the various details of the new revolutionary pattern of symbol and practice. Some events were moving directly toward the emergence of the pattern which arose in Russia. Thus happenings can be construed as transitions between one revolutionary emergent and the next one.

After the French Revolution many details of the French pattern of "democracy" were adopted and adapted. Great Britain widened the parliamentary franchise in the direction of universal suffrage. Parliaments came to exercise greater control over executives, even where revolution did not eliminate monarchial authority (as in Prussia). There were waves of land reform for the avowed benefit of peasants or small farmers; there were changes in public revenues designed to encourage commerce, industry, and finance; there was increasing use of the language of democratic internationalism.

Presently a significant political movement of protest arose in opposition to the property system which had benefited by democratic nationalism. Marxism outcompeted the "utopian" socialists and the anarchists, and furnished the dominant language in the name of which counter-elites sought to supersede the established order.

When construed with reference to the last and the next world-revolutionary patterns, the same event often possessed both revolutionary and counterrevolutionary implications. Demands for free public education and for universal suffrage often stimulated the wage earners, the peasants, and the lesser middle classes to assert themselves politically; this could be said to mark an advance toward the possible appearance of a new revolutionary impetus in the name of these classes. But some of the consequences of education and suffrage were inimical to the spread of world revolution. When concessions were made to these demands and political parties were able to obtain seats in municipal councils or national parliaments, revolutionary ardor was often lost. Party leaders became firmly incorporated in the national ideology and more intent on proving their patriotism than their proletarianism.

Correctly orientated persons living in the flow of historical happenings between the French and Russian revolutions would have seen the meaning of each situation for the spread or the restriction of these patterns of revolution.

Correct self-orientation in the world since the Russian Revolution consists in divining the meaning of current events for the passage from the last world revolution to the next one. Since we are so close to the last epochal innovation, we shall no doubt be more successful in noting the factors which influence its immediate fate than in discerning the outlines of the next significant upheaval. A search for orientation is no once-and-for-all procedure; it is a constant reappraisal of the march of time, construed self-critically with reference to possible class consequences.

We are not wholly without guidance when we undertake to construe the meaning of current affairs for the spread and restriction of the revolutionary pattern of 1917. World-revolutionary initiatives are not rare in the history of mankind, but none has ever risen to total hegemony, and unified the world in the name of one set of dominant symbols and according to one set of practices. The dialectic of restriction has proved more potent than the dialectic of diffusion, and world revolutions have always been stopped short of universality.

It will be remembered that the men of France who seized the power in the name of all humanity (*liberté, égalité, fraternité*) were not accepted by all mankind. The claims of those who seized the power in Russia to speak in the name of the world proletariat have not been accepted by all proletarians everywhere. Perhaps the same contradictions which deprived the French elite of universality in fact, despite universality in rhetoric, will operate to circumscribe the Russian elite. Evidently we have to do with a double process of diffusion and restriction.

Possibly we may guide our attention to significant aspects of the total situation by adopting certain special methods of collecting and exhibiting data. We deal with a march of time, a stream of events. By intersecting the stream at periodic intervals, and charting the geographical distribution of selected symbols and practices, we may contribute to sound understanding.

If we adopt rather wide intervals between cross sections, we may keep in contact with reality without getting lost in the sheer mass of detail. Perhaps five-year intervals will serve all the purposes in hand. Thus we may choose 1917, 1922, 1927, 1932. . . . Enough data are available to extend this five-year cross section backward between the Russian and French revolutions; were we to move further back, wider intervals would be a necessary concession to the scarcity of knowledge.

The features of the revolutionary pattern of 1917 may be briefly summarized here. Some of the positively sentimentalized words (plus symbols) were:

republic   proletariat
soviet   world revolution
socialist   communism

Some of the negatively sentimentalized words (minus symbols) were:

monarchy   imperialism
religion   parliamentarism
bourgeoisie   bourgeois liberalism
capitalism   and democracy

Some of the practices, not all of which were initiated at the beginning:

governmentalization (of organized social life)
equalization (of money income)
monopolization (of legality by a single party)

At any given cross section through the stream of events the extent of diffusion and restriction would be shown. Such relationships may be classified as follows:

Total diffusion
Restriction by geographical differentiation
Restriction by partial incorporation
Restriction by functional differentiation.

Total diffusion would be indicated by universal membership in the Soviet Union, and in the adherence of the Soviet Union to the symbols and practices proclaimed and inaugurated in 1917. Since the period of civil war and intervention, the Soviet Union has made little territorial progress, and hence total geographical diffusion has been blocked. Whether the changes which have transpired within the Soviet Union have fostered the cause of world revolution will be considered later on.

Restriction by geographical differentiation derives from ideas and propaganda emphasizing the local, parochial, provincial, circumscribed nature of the events at the center of the new revolutionary movement. The appearance of a revolutionary elite arouses the insecurities of all surrounding elites, who seek to protect themselves from external and internal menaces to their ascendancy. They seek to obtain the cooperation of their own masses against the external threat by stigmatizing it as foreign and alien, and by emphasizing their own identification with the locality. Hence a revolution in the name of humanity is treated as the *French* revolution, and a revolution in the name of the world proletariat is treated as the *Russian* revolution. The struggle to restrict the external menace emphasizes parochialism: thus the Prussian dynastic and feudal groups tolerated the language of German nationalism as a means of rallying the rank and file of the community against the French; thus the Poles and other newly independent peoples fought the Russians in 1919-1921.

Restriction by partial incorporation is the process by which successful symbols and practices of the new revolutionary regime are borrowed as a concession to local sentiment. This "me, too, but" technique of identification and distinction proceeds as follows: if "nation" is proclaimed, then let there be a peculiar essence in the "German nation"; if "socialism" be a virtue, then let it be "German National Socialism"; if "revolution" be a value, let it be our own national revolution.

The details of the revolutionary pattern which were most quickly paralleled abroad were the least novel ones. This may be shown by tabulating the changes which have occurred in the states of the world in forms of government. The overthrow of the Czar was in the best manner of the bourgeois revolutions, and similar movements went forward outside Russia, often draining off existing discontent and diminishing the chances of proletarian forms of policy. The following tables depict the situation in 1917 before the revolutionary movements of the year began. Otherwise the situation is shown as it was by the end of the year cited. Data are from such standard sources as the *Statesman's Yearbook* and the *Political Handbook of the World*. Arabi Saudi and Iraq are included for the first time in 1932. In general, colonial countries are excluded.

Year	Absolute Monarchies		Limited Monarchies		Parliamentary Monarchies		Presidential Republics		Parliamentary Republics	
	No.	%	No.	%	No.	%	No.	%	No.	%
1917	6	.10	7	.12	17	.30	21	.40	5	.08
1922	3	.05	5	.08	18	.29	21	.34	15	.24
1927	2	.04	4	.06	19	.30	22	.35	16	.25
1932	1	.02	7	.11	19	.29	21	.32	17	.26

In 1917 there were 56 states of which 13, or 22 per cent, were absolute or limited monarchies. In 1922 the number of states was 62, of which 8, or 13 per

cent, were absolute or limited monarchies. In 1927
there were 6 of 63 states, or less than 10 per cent, in
these two categories. By 1932 there were 8 of 65 states,
or 13 per cent, included. The greatest shift was toward parliamentary republics, in which are included
both soviet and nonsoviet forms. Monarchies dropped
from 52 to 42 per cent in favor of republics in the
period.

Certain of these changes are accentuated when the
forms of government are classified according to population. Figures are for the year nearest the year mentioned, when an official enumeration or estimate was
unavailable. With the exception of China, the largest
figure given in conflicting sources was used. Population is given in millions.

Year	Absolute Mon-archies		Limited Mon-archies		Parlia-mentary Mon-archies		Presi-dential Republics		Parlia-mentary Republics	
	No.	%	No.	%	No.	%	No.	%	No.	%
1917	64	.04	675	.46	171	.12	189	.13	374	.25
1922	27	.02	401	.25	203	.13	200	.13	745	.47
1927	20	.01	396	.25	215	.13	210	.13	786	.48
1932	6	.01	455	.26	210	.12	231	.13	830	.48

It thus appears that 50 per cent of the population
lived in absolute or limited monarchies in 1917. By
1922 the percentage was 27, and remained constant
in the two succeeding samples. The expansion of parliamentary republics is emphasized in this table, since
the proportion grew from one-quarter to about one-
half of the total inhabitants of states.

The more novel details of the revolutionary pattern
of 1917 have spread slowly. When the facts are as-
sembled, it will no doubt appear that the governmentalization of organized life has proceeded apace
outside the Soviet Union. This interpretation will ap-

ply if some allowance is made for the extension of governmental control during the period of the World War, comparing the situation as it was in 1912 with the transformations recorded in the postwar years. Civil emergencies connected with the great depression of 1929 have been met with notable extensions of governmental authority, even in the United States. The Reconstruction Finance Corporation was but one of the early and conspicuous examples of this trend.

In all probability there has been a general though very erratic movement toward the equalization of money income. The nonsoviet communities of Central and Eastern Europe sought to assuage popular discontent and to build up vested and sentimental support for their nonsoviet regimes by dividing up the large landed estates. Elsewhere high income and inheritance taxes have furthered tendencies toward equalization; but often such policies have been offset by higher exactions upon articles of general consumption. "Share the Wealth" has become a practical political slogan in the United States.

The monopolization of legality by a single dominant party is found in Germany, Italy, and in less evolved form in such countries as China, Turkey, and Yugoslavia.

Evidently, therefore, restrictions by geographical differentiation and by partial incorporation have made rapid headway in limiting the scope of the Soviet Union. To these processes may be added restriction by functional differentiation. The history of the past century shows that a turning point in political development was reached when it became common to refer to the French Revolution as the "bourgeois" revolution. The language which had been used by the original revolutionary elite of France was universalist in scope. By referring to the revolution as the "bourgeois" revolution, it was both implied and asserted that a special class had used the name of the many for the advantage of the few. Not all mankind, but the bourgeoisie were those who were supposed to have reaped most of the benefits which accrued from the dramatic events of the years following 1789.

A distinction of this kind strikes at the basic claim of the revolutionary order, challenges the dominant myth, exposes its fraudulent pretensions. Every elite which has become identified with any of the symbols and practices of the last revolution is indicted. The symbolic foundation is laid for a new revolutionary edifice; the new mythology of protest, the new utopian promise, can be invoked against the ideologies of the established elites. In the terminology of the nineteenth century the alternative to the "bourgeoisie" was the "proletariat." With the perfection of Marxist socialism a new formative myth was set loose, to gain allegiance during successive pulsations of discontent, and culminate when the bearers of the new symbols seized the power in Russia.

Have lines of functional differentiation begun to cast doubt upon the universality of the Russian Revolution? Are there those who doubt whether the class consequences of the revolution benefit the whole proletariat as much as they benefit certain other class formations?

Perhaps, as some anarchosyndicalists have suggested, the lower layers of the manual workers, especially the unemployed, have been grossly misled by the sloganeering of the spokesmen of the Russian Revolution. Perhaps the rise of modern political socialism is a phase in the struggle for power, not of the manual workers, but of the "intellectuals" who successfully allied themselves with the discontented manual workers in wresting power from the aristocracy and the plutocracy. Once established in power, they give special privileges to special skill, capturing party and administration. Deference and higher money incomes go to those who perform technical and organizational functions, not to those who do manual work. Intellectuals have demonstrated that Marx did not really intend to establish mechanical equality of money income. Hence the lowest layers of the population, possessed of less skill than the upper layers, are potential sources of disaffection, suspicion of "bureaucracy."

This line of analysis views the Russian Revolution as an incident in the rise to power of the lesser bourgeoisie, a Russian realization of the tendencies which are implicit in the march of events in Italy, Germany, and elsewhere.

It may be that the common factor in the seeming political confusion of our time is the rise to power of the middle-income skill group. Despite the contradictions and the aberrations of Russian Communism, Italian Fascism, and German National Socialism, a new world revolution may be on the march which will be realized independently of the inclusion of the world within the Soviet Union. In the name of the "nation's workers," and in the name of local patriotism, of antiforeignism, middle-income skill groups are rising to power at the expense of aristocracy and plutocracy.

Plainly the middle-income skill groups have not yet found a common name; nor have they discerned the inner principle of sacrifice on which their unity depends; nor have they risen to the full comprehension of their historic destiny. In Europe their disunion has bred the politics of catastrophe; but in America there may be more time for the attainment of a common name, a common policy, and a common sense of political destiny,

Lacking self-consciousness, the small farmers, the small businessmen, the low-salaried intellectuals, and the skilled workers have fought one another rather than acted together. The labor movements of the nineteenth and twentieth centuries have in many ways intensified rather than resolved the contradictions within the middle-income skill group. One element of the middle-income skill group has catered to the wage earners; it is composed of trades-union organizers, trades-union editors, trades-union secretaries, Socialist party organizers, Socialist party secretaries, and officials in cooperative societies. Such functionaries are often "renegades" from the older middle-income skill formations; their fathers may have been merchants, farmers, teachers, officials. Others rise from the ranks of the manual workers, learning to elude physical toil by cultivating oratorical skill, literary ability, and administrative technique.

The older middle-income groups have hated with deep intensity the skill group of proletarian origin or affiliation. One basis of this is the sense of outrage that those who exercise the same skill should get ahead by simple differences in vocabulary. The tool of preacher, teacher, lawyer, and journalist is the larynx and not the biceps. When fellow toilers of the tongue and typewriter ensconce themselves on pay rolls by saying "bourgeoisie" with a hiss and "proletariat" with a flaunt, resentment turns to bitterness and curdles into indignation.

All this seemed profoundly hypocritical to the older bourgeoisie, and insult is added to injury when the spokesmen of the proletariat indict this group as the tools of the exploiter. It is easy to understand why the National Socialists, when they seized power in Germany, swept official swivels free of "Communists," "Social Democrats," and "Democrats," and packed them off to concentration camps. In their place ruled men more closely identified with the older middle-income groups, but called "National Socialists."

Such intense inner strife is one mark of a social formation which has not yet come to itself, and attained full class consciousness. It lacks a consistent policy, a rallying name, and an invigorating myth of its historic mission. Quite typically, the energies of the middle-income skill group in America have been diverted toward the restriction of slavery and the restriction of thriftlessness by efforts to remove al-

cohol, gambling, and prostitution. Waves of indignation at the inequitable results of industrial concentration have been dissipated in struggles to regulate
"unfair competition" and to obtain "easy credit."
Farmers and small businessmen on the receding fron-
tier followed the spell of "16 to 1," "antimonopoly,"
and the "new freedom"; but the principal effect of
efforts to "restore competition" has been to complicate
corporations. The lesser agrarian, business, professional, and skilled worker elements are left with no
common body of effective political symbols.

The energy expended in Bryanism, Rooseveltianism,
and Wilsonism might have organized sentiment
around symbols capable of clarifying the special demands of the middle-income skill group. It is thinkable
that during these many years the low-income farmers,
storekeepers, schoolteachers, and clergymen might
have learned to demand the rigorous use of the national taxing power to eliminate immoderate incomes.
Had they become acquainted with the fact that America was run by a single party system, they might have
ceased to divide their potential majority of ballots
between the Republican and Democratic wings of the
Republocratic party.

As it stands today the middle-income group is bereft
of so much as an acknowledged name capable of distinguishing it from the proletariat and the plutocracy.
There is something repugnant to the individualism
of the middle class about the name "middle class."
Apt for analysis, it is inept for propaganda. In order
to distinguish themselves from the "alien" proletariat,
the middle-income skill groups have warmed to such
ambiguous expressions as "citizen," "American," "pa-
triot," used by demagogues who were often sustained
from behind the scenes by the bigger industrial, commercial, and financial interests.

Lacking an inspiring name and clear demands for
national policy, the middle-income skill group has no
myth of its virtues and its destiny. It can be contended

that the bond which unites this class is both external and internal: external, since it loses monetary rewards to the plutocracy; internal, since sacrifice for the sake of obtaining socially useful skill is a common experience of moral worth. Self-discipline is involved in the acquisition of skill through specialized training, which is a basis of mutual esteem among mechanics, intellectuals, and enterprisers.

The middle-income skill group in various nations might conceive of its historic mission in these terms: to recapture the initiative in the struggle for social justice. In the eighteenth century the mission of the middle-income skill group was to collaborate with all comers in breaking the chains of feudal-monarchical society, and seeking to establish the principle of proportionality between sacrifice and reward.

During the nineteenth and twentieth centuries the expansion of modern industrialism has created a plutocracy, whose presence shows that the balance between sacrifice and reward has been drastically disturbed. Once more the political "destiny" of the middle-income skill group is plain: it is the remoralization of society by changing the practices of society in regard to reward and sacrifice.

As the middle-income skill group attains the dignity and insight of an effective social formation, it will see that it has been the victim of a psychological lag. The middle-income skill group has stayed loyal to the vocabulary of individualism after the practices sustained by this vocabulary generated great discrepancies between sacrifice and reward.

Despite every handicap, it might be argued that the middle-income skill group is on the way to ultimate victory. The implacable processes of commercial, industrial, and financial capitalism have stimulated it to political activity. It may be that the middle-income skill group has suffered no absolute decline in material income, but there is no mistaking the decline in psychological income, in deference. The skill groups, especially the older ones, have been harried on one side by the organized agencies which spoke in the name of the proletariat, and on the other by the powerful combines of the plutocracy.

In Germany there were superimposed upon the psychological losses of a century, the adversities of war, defeat, inflation, and depression. Goaded to desperation, the older middle-income elements rose to partial self-realization in the National Socialist movement, even supplying their own leadership in the person of Hitler, son of a small customs official formerly in the service of the Hapsburgs. The Italian Fascist movement had already been used by a man who had previously made his living by employing the vocabulary of "proletarian" protest. Mussolini may be a renegade in the sense that in adult life he altered his political convictions and persecuted his former friends, but in a class sense Mussolini was a prodigal son returning to his own.

Plainly the Italian and German movements are incidents in the process by which the last world-revolutionary pattern is both restricted and universalized. The domination of Moscow is decisively rejected; but it would be a mistake to suppose that revolution itself is dead. Restriction has proceeded by taking over some of the symbols and practices of the new pattern, even as the French revolutionary pattern spread after the emphatic rejection of the authority of the French to administer the revolution.

This treatment of the Russian Revolution as the "Second Bourgeois Revolution" may foster the march to power of middle-income skill groups in other countries though not under the command of Moscow. It may also deflate the pretensions of the Russian revolutionary movement to invoke the name of the proletariat. The anarchosyndicalist appeal to the manual workers to rise against the bureaucratic state may embody the germ of the next great revolutionary upheaval "from underneath"; every indication is that this appeal will prove ineffectual in any visible future, while the "skill revolution" gradually will move toward universality.

This chapter has developed the implications of the view that political events may be seen as the passage from the dominance of one class form to the next. The French Revolution marked the rise of the bourgeoisie; the Russian Revolution may mark the rise of the lesser bourgeoisie, the skill groups. The next major revolutionary impulsion may come in the name of the manual workers against the bureaucratic state fostered by socialism. Meanwhile, the scope of the elite which seized authority in Russia is being circumscribed by the same processes which restricted the scope of the elite in revolutionary France. The main features of the new revolutionary pattern, however, continue to move toward universality, though in a disunited world.

PERSONALITY

What is the significance of social life for the survival of forms of political personality? In some respects this query about politics is closer to everyday attitudes in an individualistic society than is analysis by class or skill. Who has not dramatized politics as a struggle between Stalin and Trotsky, Roosevelt and Hoover? Whether the stakes are exile or dictatorship, presidency or private life, Washington or the old home town, the players are identifiable persons, and their fate is humanly exciting.

However, it is not the fate of the individual Tom, Dick, and Harry that holds our interest. Political analysis is more concerned with the general than with the unique. Our task is to examine the factors affecting success or failure of personality type. The Franklins, Benitos, Adolfs, and Josefs must be seen as instances of more general forms of personal development before we can compare them with predecessors, contemporaries, and successors.

Novelists, poets, and painters have long been preoccupied with the delicate nuances which bind men to one another, or condemn them to stare across seemingly impassable chasms of misunderstanding. Behind the façades of the class and skill struggle run the dialectics of personality. In the *Brothers Karamazov* are depicted the subtler shades of the subjective which divide one person, and one personality, from another. The modern student has sought to illuminate this obscure terrain in the language of exposition rather than depiction. Such expository works as those of Freud, Klages, Jung, and Kretschmer have become part of the common inheritance of cultivated men and women throughout Western European civilization.

Political life, in the narrowest sense of the word, is a life of conflict, and presupposes men who can bring themselves into active relationship to their surroundings. Impulses must be externalized upon the human environment. A fully developed political personality combines certain motives with certain skills, fusing an emotional capacity to externalize impulses with enough skill to secure success.

This requirement of externalized impulse at once eliminates from the arena of rough-and-tumble politics certain personalities who have failed to achieve an emotional life sufficiently free to enable them to express themselves in the world of reality. Witness the disintegrated wrecks who lie in the wards of institutions for the care of sufferers from severe mental disease. In some of these cases the evidence is convincing that systems of motivation within the personality clashed so decisively with other systems of motivation within the same personality that the whole energy of the individual was absorbed in the inner struggle, leaving nothing over for the task of remaining orientated toward surroundings. Such individuals may spend days and weeks quite motionless, seemingly oblivious to all beyond themselves.

Such pathological pictures of complete internalization offer the greatest possible contrast to the active political figure. The politician displaces his private motives upon public objects, and rationalizes the displacement in terms of public advantage. When this emotional and symbolic adjustment occurs in combination with facility in the acquisition of manipulative skill, the effective politician emerges.

Some of the problems connected with the synthesis of motive and skill involved in politics may be broached by considering the behavior of Abraham Lincoln during his mature years. Lincoln was firm in his public pronouncements and in his official acts, revealing a flexible capacity to adjust his tactics to the changing features of reality. He remained in strong though not in domineering control of the situation. He may be contrasted with Stanton, his secretary of war, whose tenacity and energy were so often tinged with sadism; with McClellan, the general who never felt quite prepared to fight, and whose unwillingness to proceed under pressure was not firmness but negativism, nourished by unconscious fear; or with Greeley, fiery journalist, who fathered many chimerical expedients.

Inseparable from the public picture of Lincoln was his gentleness. His clemency was famous everywhere and notorious among his colleagues. Those who came in closer contact with Lincoln saw that he was over-gentle and lacking in firmness in intimate relationships. They saw how incapable he was of disciplining his own children, and how overindulgent he was of his exigent wife. The true measure of this gentleness was its continuation despite provocation. Very rarely did Lincoln allow flares of indignation to escape him. But once an officer who tried to "bulldoze" the President into granting his petition scornfully said, "I see you have made up your mind against doing me justice!" Lincoln's face convulsed with pain, and he is said to have grabbed the officer by the collar and unceremoniously bundled him out of the room.

His sadness impressed contemporaries, who saw the brooding brows, the sunken cheeks, the luminous eyes, the deliberate ways; and they saw his tears at Gettysburg. Those who knew Lincoln intimately found that sadness was one of the many evidences of depression; Lincoln was plagued by insomnia, feelings of inferiority, of bearing too much responsibility, of pessimism. At times the President was suicidal. During the battle of Chancellorsville when it appeared that General Hooker was in retreat, Stanton says that Lincoln threw up his hands and exclaimed, "My God! Stanton, our cause is lost! This is more than I can endure!" The President later said that he had fully made up his mind to end his life in the Potomac River.

Lincoln's sadness was sometimes relieved by wit, often in the homely form which offended the cultivated and delighted the rustic. His extreme devotion to duty cut him off more and more from intimate human contacts. His honesty, and his desire to deal with scrupulous justice with his fellows were obvious. Allied to patience and gentleness was toleration of personal criticism. And of course Lincoln's physical courage was not in question.

Without summing up in detail the manifold personality of the man, but pausing to consider the principal features, we cannot fail to be impressed by the discrepancy between his firmness in relation to technical objects (his public duties) and his dependent, passively enduring attitude toward his wife. It is clear, also, that Lincoln spent a great deal of his energy in antiself reactions, which ranged all the way from gloomy moods and depressing fantasies to the contemplation of suicide. The melancholy tinge of his waking life stands in stark contrast to the subjective tone of men who have few morbid moments and who live in serene self-assurance. Plainly much of Lincoln's great energy was not externally effective in dealing with his environment, but turned back against the personality; and much of the energy which was internalized took the form of morbid rather than grandiose reverie.

There is ample evidence of Lincoln's craving for the approval of a wide public. When the news of Chancellorsville burst upon him, his reaction was not only "Our cause is lost!" but the question, "What will the people say?" Many another chief executive has lived through moments of apparent disaster without exhibiting so much dependence upon public sentiment, and without being moved to suicidal plans when public approval seemed lost.

Much of Lincoln's personality was a defense formation against extreme demands for wide appreciation. By tempering his conduct with incessant thoughts of the just rather than the popular, by neglecting as far as possible to take note of the avalanches of criticism which poured upon him, Lincoln was able to erect buffers against his own yearning for constant appreciation.

What of the conditions in which such personality type rise to eminence? Lincoln won the presidential nomination from Seward largely because his language was less peremptory than Seward's. When the Republican party met in convention, there was no doubt of the personal popularity of Seward. But the party wanted to win the election, and there were the doubtful states of New Jersey, Pennsylvania, Indiana, and Illinois to be taken into consideration. Against the outspoken Seward the Republicans would be at a disadvantage in dealing with the Democratic candidate, Douglas. Seward had appealed to the "higher law" above the Constitution. This was profoundly shocking at this stage of the developing crisis; it seemed to indicate an imperious determination to force the issue. The Northern states were divided among themselves. Quite apart from constitutional issues, antislavery sentiment was not unanimous. Lincoln had distinguished himself by firmness; yet he had spoken in terms which somewhat veiled the grimness of the crisis. Lincoln had talked of "moral codes" to supplement legal ones. As one of his biographers, L. Pierce Clark, wrote: "The principles of the two views are identical, but Lincoln knows how so to state the principle that it alarms few, although many must know that they are not essentially different." Lincoln was less ruthless and peremptory, more conciliatory and winning, than Seward; at this phase of crisis, his personality was more acceptable.

After winning the election, Lincoln gradually led the Northern states to a united front against secession and slavery. It was his capacity to chasten destructive drives, to temper them to reality, or to turn them against himself, that was well adapted to the situation. The Northern States, torn by local, regional, denominational, and other differences, edged rather than rushed toward the approaching war. The Southerners, unified in the name of "our sacred institutions," strode forward to meet the crisis. Lincoln's mixture of firmness and gentleness alternately commanded and wheedled the Northerners into unified action.

The chances are that Lincoln would not have found his way to the top if the North had been a united rather than a divided people. Certainly the Southern leadership contained few figures of the Lincoln stamp. United people are peremptory when attacked. As heterogeneous people become more united during crises, they become more ruthless, partly as a reaction against previous doubts and scruples. Conciliatory personalities tend to be swept aside as indecisive weaklings. Lincoln, it will be remembered, narrowly missed defeat in 1864.

It is correct to say that Lincoln was an agitator in the sense that he displaced strong cravings for emotional response from the intimate circle to the wider public, and that he acquired enough skill in oral and written discourse to succeed. He was not, however, restricted to a purely agitational role, for, unlike Greeley, for example, he was able to hold his destructive impulses in sufficient restraint to permit him to coordinate the efforts of others in organization.

Suppose we undertake to explain the type of development that was displayed by Lincoln. Three questions present themselves at once. Under what conditions is the demand for love displaced from the primary to the secondary public? Under what conditions is there extreme demand for love? When are aggressive impulses held in check and partially turned against the self?

The displacement of strong demands for response from the intimate to the wider public is favored by failure in the intimate sphere. We have seen that Lincoln's marriage was not an emotional success, and if we go further into his history, we discover that Lincoln exhibited some difficulties in relation to women. He left Mary Todd waiting at the altar on the "fatal first of January, 1841," plunging into a depression which was so serious that physicians still differ in diagnosing this reaction as neurotic or psychotic. Lincoln went into serious depression when Ann Rutledge died; and, further back than that, he suffered severely when his mother died when he was nine years old. Although shy and ineffectual with women of his own age, he got on with maternal women who were usually older than himself. His displacement onto the political public can be attributed to the focusing of his attention upon political activity in the environment where he was reared.

What was the origin of the great demand for love, which, since it could not be resolved in the primary sphere, was partly resolved by displacement? When we have to do with a living person who is willing to try to understand himself by the method of free association (psychoanalysis), by saying everything that comes into his mind, we are able to learn a great deal about early formative experiences. Many old and long-forgotten episodes are recalled, many old impulses are rediscovered. This method is unavailable for the study of Lincoln, of course; but psychoanalysts have often

studied personalities who display the chief characteristics of Lincoln's life.

It is found that when the young child is overindulged by his mother in nursing, or in handling his
body, the child may display great unwillingness to re-
linquish his demands to be nursed. Urges to incor-
porate objects through the mouth, to be dependent,
to be cared for, to remain inactive, may become very
powerful. Hence the individual stays relatively fixated
upon early ways of reacting to the world, and en-
counters many difficulties in subsequent development.
In ensuing crises the individual is prone to regress to
this early fixation and to remain immature.

Lincoln's early environment was in some respects
emotionally unstable. His father was often harsh and
often overindulgent; this type of contradictory treatment arouses great uncertainties about being loved.
There is no evidence that young Lincoln responded to
the obstacles put in his way by his father by growing
intractable. Nor is there any evidence that he gave
up the struggle and retired completely within himself.
But there is ample indication that Lincoln had strong
tendencies to regress when difficulties presented themselves in his pathway. It is recorded that throughout
his entire life the dream of a ship recurred when crises
were intense. This dream is of a pattern which has
often been met and described in our civilization for
similar persons under similar circumstances.

In general, we can think of behavior as a system of
acts which are running toward completion at varying
rates along different channels. A completed act is a
sequence of events running from impulse through sub-
jectivity to expression, and to the reinstatement of a
situation very like the situation before the impulse got
under way. Thus hunger contractions may be followed
and accompanied by the subjective sense of hunger,
and by nursing, which completes the act by abolishing hunger contractions. The infantile organism is
equipped to complete some acts, like sucking, swal-

lowing, and defecating. When these acts are interfered with, substitutions may occur, or persistence and rage reactions may appear. If persistence and rage reactions are not successful in removing the obstacle, such reactions may be turned against the personality itself, establishing an internal resistance to the completion of the impulses in question. By this process a rigorous system of inhibition and compulsion may be developed.[1]

The mother or nurse not only indulges the infant and the young child, but denies; hence the mother is both "good" and "bad" to the child (whose attitude is thus ambivalent). The basis of depression is laid when the child is deprived of the loved one (as by death), and responds regressively, that is, by seeking to substitute fantasy for reality. The "good" mother is fondly remembered as the perfectly indulgent mother; but at the same time the rage at the "bad" mother is turned against the self. Hence the individual in extreme cases punishes a part of his personality on behalf of another part of his personality. When children undergo great deprivations during phases of great ambivalence, they often respond through this depressive mechanism. Subsequently they love persons after the ambivalent patterns of infancy, and if they are not constantly supplied with love, rage gets the upper hand, but this rage is internalized in the form of depression and perhaps even suicide.

Just why does this internalizing occur? Because of acute fear of loss. The fear may be precipitated by fear of physical retaliation, by fear of losing future love, by

[1] For technical purposes the original patterns of expression may be called libidinal channels; persistence and rage reactions may be called ego channels; other patterns may be named transformations. The transformations include total repression, partial repression, identification, projection, masochism, detachment, and several other reactions which will not be discussed here. For details, see the standard treatises by Sigmund Freud.

fear of being treated with contempt. Failure in the tactics of persistence and rage may have occurred; but the urges toward defiance, though subdued, are not relinquished. A strong structure of inhibition is constantly in conflict with potent impulses. Such persons are overshy or even overconscientious. Lincoln, it will be recalled, was famous for his overscrupulous honesty. Rarely did the underlying destructive tendencies break through to external manifestations. We know only of Lincoln's extremely sadistic attacks on Shields, and perhaps his damaging anonymous letters to the Grigsbys (their authenticity is in dispute).

Evidently, then, we must class Lincoln among the partially inhibited rage types. The relatively uninhibited rage types usually come into such incessant conflict with other people that they play little part in political activity. They are extremely willful, violent, domineering, and egocentric. The child who is accustomed to tantrums and to violence as a means of responding to denial may get little love at adolescence, and strengthen tendencies to remain resentfully fixed on primitive ways of dealing with the world. The uninhibited rage types are able to accomplish something by intimidation, but they are constantly encountering difficulty because of defensive behavior on the part of society. Many of these uninhibited rage types contribute to the ranks of the aggressive delinquent, unemployable and criminal.

Success in cowing the environment by willfulness forms a personality predisposed toward imperious violence. The first Napoleon appears to have won through willfulness from the second year of his life. He grew into a quarrelsome and combative child; and when his parents, seeking to curb his truculence, sent him to a girls' school at the age of five, he was only spoiled by his teachers and schoolmates, who tolerated the eccentricities of the only boy among them. Evidently Napoleon was deeply fixated on the mother imago, and resentful of the rivalry of his elder brother Joseph, whom he used to "thump and bite." His inordinate craving for deference was but partly gratified, even by success; for the picture of an inferior self, against which he struggled, was ever with him. Among his companions at the military school at Brienne he felt hopelessly inferior, for he was but five feet five in height. He was taunted as poor and Corsican. He secretly worried lest his sexual organs were atrophied, and lived an active sexual life as a constant means of reassuring himself of his doubtful masculinity. But throughout his life Napoleon was subject to moods of melancholy and to reveries of inferiority and isolation. To some extent these were mitigated by fantasies and claims to grandiosity: "I am no ordinary man, and laws of propriety and morals are not applicable to me." But he was haunted by exaggerated fears of a conspirative environment. In fundamental respects Napoleon was very close to the true political type. With his insatiable craving for gestures of deference to his ego from his fellow men, he had no durable interests in the objective processes of nature or the conditions of beauty. He sought the balm of success for his wounded ego, and he was forever licking his self-inflicted mutilations.

The inhibited rage types are often relieved of their inhibitions upon destructiveness during collective crises. They are prone to fortify their personalities by allying themselves with collectively acceptable symbols and practices. Hence they can play parts in political movements which are closed to the ill-tempered, uncontrolled, impatient rage types.

There is a rather completely inhibited rage type which is depicted in the popular phrase about a child "whose will is broken." Aggressive tendencies are disavowed by this personality, which treats the environment itself as overwhelmingly dangerous; hence the excessive timidity.

The partially inhibited rage group may be strongly masochistic. By enduring much mental anguish Lincoln was able to permit the expression of his aggressive impulses in the chastened form of firmness without accumulating a disastrous load of hampering guilt. The suffering expiated the guilt and released the impulse for expression. His apparent suffering won the sympathy of some who knew him intimately, and who felt impelled to minister to the protection of one who endured such inner anguish. True masochists are avid for affection, and, as Karen Horney has emphasized, they often use physical sexuality and experiences of intimate indulgence as means of being reassured against the anxieties generated by efforts to down the profoundly destructive components of their natures.

Such extremely masochistic types are often devoted to aggressive personalities who externalize their own aggressions. The entourage of every dominating leader is likely to contain such masochistic individuals who perform conscientious service to the "chief" and the "cause."

Another major mode of dealing with inner stress is detachment, which was also to some extent involved in the complex personality of Lincoln. Extreme detachment may be exhibited by conduct which seems to be "inhuman." The individual in question may be polite but never spontaneous. A thin barrier of barely perceptible ice freezes more expressive natures.

Excessive detachment marked the personality of a chemist who became entangled in practical politics rather by accident. He was known to his associates as exceptionally gifted in mathematics and experimental science. In personal relations he was quiet, soft spoken, gentle, polite, and acquiescent. Those who knew him best sensed that his inner life was tinged with no high light of enthusiasm, depression, rage, or love. He seemed to meet the world with poise and equanimity. He came to the attention of the police when he lay stunned by an explosion in the "bomb factory" which he ran for his revolutionary friends. Psychoanalytic interviews disclosed that he cared very little for the revolutionary philosophy of his associates. He ran the "bomb factory" as a side line, partly because he was interested in the technical problems involved, and partly because he wanted to be agreeable to his friends.

An important disclosure was made early in these interviews, however. He said that he had been seized by an irresistible impulse to hurl a bomb through the window of his laboratory and to destroy the whole building. Almost as if he were in a dream he had gone to the window overlooking the courtyard, thrown the bomb, which exploded prematurely and demolished the adjacent rooms.

Later on he recalled that on some previous occasions the same imperative impulse to destroy had seized control of him. Once when climbing an Alpine peak, he had noticed the reverie that if the rock by his hand were but slightly jarred, it would roll down the mountain and hit the next man beneath him. Some strange force seemed to take possession of his hand, which detached the rock, and his companion fell to death. The chemist felt no shock, but mild wonder. There was no feeling that the destructive impulse belonged to his own personality.

In extreme cases of "emotionlessness" the person often has a well-developed "spectator self" which seems to observe his own mental processes without feeling any sense of being personally involved. If such personalities figure in politics, it is usually as theorists or by accident.

The personality of Lincoln has often been contrasted with a persecutory agitator like Greeley. The basis of the Greeley type is probably the extensive use of projection and displacement as ways of coping with guilty and hostile tendencies. Such agitators share the common failure to obtain sufficient indulgence in relation to intimate objects, and transfer this craving to an enlarged world of objects. They succeed in externalizing their assertive impulses by projecting an inner sense of guilt upon the world outside; if the world is in the wrong, they are in the right by attacking it. The precarious nature of this adjustment is often shown by its collapse in adversity. When Greeley, for instance, suffered property losses and political defeat late in life, he developed a severe melancholia. His aggressions came tumbling back against the self, and he ceased to figure in the world of action.

Certain personalities are distinguished by haughty rather than persecutory behavior. The analysis of haughty people has often disclosed the functional basis of haughty behavior in the struggle against self contempt. By displacing contempt for the self upon the environment, and treating the world as contemptible, the personality is enabled to reduce the inner crisis. When a child is struggling for control of his excretions, verbal methods are often used to express disdain. To "smell bad" is to be treated with aversion, to be shamed. The tendency to accept the "you smell bad" as the correct self-valuation struggles with the tendency to project the valuation upon the environment. By haughtily treating the environment as foul smelling, self-esteem is often retained.[2]

Another way to resolve the stresses which arise from inhibited destructive impulses is to act obsessively and compulsively. Such reactions range all the way from Stanton, who amazed everybody by his fanatical devotion to work, which he carried on with concentrated

[2] More vindictive, parsimonious, and secretive tendencies are connected with resentment at the interferences of the nurse with fecal and urethral indulgences. Infants and children may obstinately cling to pleasure in the retention of feces, and resent violations of privacy and urgings to adhere to routine.

intensity, bad temper, and cruelty, to the behavior of bureaucrats and ceremonializers who handcuff themselves in ritualistic repetitiousness. Hounded by destructive tendencies, they hold them in abeyance by means of order, red tape, routine, stereotype. The destructive impulses receive expression by annoying, exasperating, and rebuffing the world.

Some forms of extraverted personalities respond excitedly to the mood of the moment. The study of such personalities reveals a shallow subjective life. Often the individual passes suddenly between hyperactivity in relation to business, sex, or sociality, and great depression, lassitude, and sleep. Noisy and insistent promotional types often come from these extraverted personalities. They usually prove insensitive to the reactions of others, failing to detect boredom, handling persons as if they were things classified into a small number of simple categories. Deeper study often reveals acute developmental crises which were resolved by flight into extraversion.

It appears to be well established that philosophers and other elaborate thinkers about nature and the world are usually recruited from inhibited types. Alexander Herzberg collected intimate data about thirty world-famous philosophers in *The Psychology of Philosophers*. Most of them had been hesitant in embarking on a career, and were inefficient in their occupations. Most of them were unwilling or unable to earn money. The married life of the philosophers showed conspicuous peculiarities: fifteen of the thirty did not marry at all, six married very late, four were unhappily married, two separated from their mates. Most of them were diffident in social intercourse or unsuited to it. Herzberg found that they were equally inept in politics. Plato made abortive attempts to exercise practical influence, and Aristotle lost favor. Bacon was disgraced for accepting bribes, and Mill suffered many setbacks. Hume was the great exception. As secretary and later as deputy to the British ambassador in Paris, and finally as undersecretary of state, he was very successful. All these men seemed to possess a vigorous impulsive life which they had inhibited by consciences so stern that their efforts to cope with immediate reality were cramped; hence the resort to thought.

Since we have seen that many active politicians were driven by potent consciences, we may inquire after the factors which determine whether philosophy, neurosis, or politics will result. As far as can be judged from inadequate data, agitators are the politicians who have most in common with philosophers. The early environment was undependable. In the main the environment was very indulgent during formative years, but this indulgence was subject to interruption by sudden deprivations. An unstable relation between the parents in the home may have meant that the pleasant emotional weather was subject to upsetting storms; hence the child learned to respond sensitively to the changing barometer of human attitudes.

It is plain that severe crises may resolve the inner difficulties of the individual, freeing his inhibited impulses to express themselves on the world outside himself. Shy and timid boys who survive the harrowing experiences of shellfire have suddenly blossomed out into calm, bold, and masterful persons. The anxieties were "abreacted" and overcome.

When crises intensify in the direction of violence, uninhibited rage types find more social sanction for the discharge of their sadistic drives; inhibited rage types, relieved somewhat of retaliatory fear, give greater scope to their aggressive tendencies; healthily assertive types resort to ruthlessness, though less tinctured with overactive cruelty and vindictiveness. During the initial phases of crisis, emotional solutions occur at different rates in different places. Conciliatory personalities are popular where indecision is bred of heterogeneity. They are passed over when imperious unity has been attained. In the aftermath of crisis, less dictatorial types rise in the scale of popularity.

The insecurities of the contemporary world, sharpened by the vicissitudes of a rapidly expanding and rapidly contracting economy, foster the conditions of perpetual crisis which favor the seizure of power by the agitator, and the retention of power by the man of ruthless violence.

NINE

ATTITUDE

What is the meaning of social life for the political attitudes of successive elites? Plainly very different personality forms may share the same political outlook and belong to the same elite. At one time the predominating attitudes may be "local," "regional," "national," or "international." At another time the ruling attitudes may be loyalty to "class" or "skill." Under some conditions the ruling groups are "militant"; often they are "conciliatory." Politics is a changing pattern of loyalties, strategies, tactics; and political analysis may quite properly review the succession of predominant attitudes through the stream of time.

Acts of the most acute political interest are acts which change the social environment. Political acts are therefore externalized acts, since they implicate the environment as they run to completion. Internalized acts involve only the organism itself. If we observe any individual through a given period of time, we may perceive that he stimulates his personal environment, and that he in turn is directly stimulated by this environment. There is no doubt that his acts are *object orientations*. But if an individual is out of touch with the immediate situation for five minutes, we may be in some indecision about the nature of his subjective reactions. He may be solving a problem which will culminate in relevant action in some future situation. If so, his thought is *adjustive*. But it may be that he is plunged in gloomy meditation on his own deficiencies, merely intensifying the mood of depression and initiating no activity which would rectify his relationship to the world. His reveries would then be *autistic* (preoccupied with self). Yet another important reaction may be displayed by the subject of study. He may become incapacitated for love or work by stomach troubles, skin afflictions, or headaches which have no lesional basis. Such responses are *somatic* (bodily) *conversions*.

The four forms of reaction just sketched may be recapitulated thus:

> Object orientation
> Adjustive thought
> Autistic reverie
> Somatic conversion.

Politicians often show marked changes in their behavior which may be tersely described in these terms. When Mr. X, member of Congress, lost an election, he promptly established a new relationship to the world of practical politics by becoming a lawyer-lobbyist in Washington. When his wife died, he promptly married again. Other men have met similar reverses in professional and intimate life by withdrawing from immediate reality and devoting themselves to creative research or writing. A frustrated political career is responsible for the diversion of Machiavelli's energy into history and political science. Other men have reacted to rebuff by becoming incapacitated through reverie or bodily ailment. A certain councilman would grow depressed whenever he lost an election, refuse to eat, and retire to a sanitarium, where he elaborated morbid reveries of suicide. His friends would run him for office again, and when elected he would promptly forsake his difficulties and function as efficiently as usual. Still another councilman would develop gall bladder and similar troubles when he was rejected at the polls.

Politics is itself often a substitute reaction which comes about because of deprivations in other spheres of life. Brigadier General Ezra Mannon in Eugene O'Neill's *Mourning Becomes Electra* discloses himself to his wife in these words:

Maybe you've always known you didn't love me. I call to mind the Mexican War. I could see you wanted me to go. I had a feeling you'd grown to hate me . . . That was why I went. I was hoping I might get killed. Maybe you were hoping that too. . . . When I came back you had turned to your new baby, Orin. . . . I turned to Vinnie, but a daughter's not a wife. Then I made up my mind I'd do my work in the world and leave you alone in your life and not care. That's why the shipping wasn't enough—why I became a judge and a mayor and such vain truck, and why folks in town look on me as so able! Ha!

In a biography of Joseph II, Saul K. Padover has shown the effect upon Joseph of the death of his wife, Isabel of Parma, an experience which was embittered by the discovery that his melancholy wife had never loved him. Thenceforth Joseph II was "hard, dry, and bitter," wholly immersed in administration, and harsh, cold, and contemptuous of women. In the incisive phrase of Casanova, even the face of Joseph expressed "conceit and suicide."

Even an indulgent environment does not always elicit uniform reactions. A promotion may release a whole new burst of activity; the new office manager may brim with new ideas and take a wife. The success of one book may stimulate a stream of books from the author. But sometimes the responses to success are singularly disproportionate. The individual may develop grave doubts of his own ability, grow gloomy and depressed. He may develop physical symptoms, or indulge in the excessive use of drugs. Or he may grow arrogant, peremptory, cruel, thus preparing the way for final failure. Freud was able to describe types who collapse when success comes. He found that they were often driven by unconscious guilt feelings when confronted by an opportunity to take the role of authority, to give orders, to demand attention.

It is possible to put individual incidents of the sort just named into the wider context of events in which they occur. Each deprivation and indulgence, each form of response is paralleled in any community by other incidents of the same kind, or deviates atypically from them. We can isolate sequences which are characteristic of particular groups.

Unemployment, for example, is a frequent deprivation which every community in the modern world inflicts upon its members. Individual responses run through the entire gamut of internalized and externalized solutions. There may be morbid self-accusations of failure, leading to suicide; or physical difficulties of functional origin may develop. There may be growing preoccupation with fantasy in the form of daydreams, adventure stories, or motion-picture romances. There may be private reading in order to learn new skills which will prove useful if new opportunities open up. There may also be serious reading and study devoted to economic conditions; this may lead up to express demands for overt changes in the real environment.

To some extent blocked assertive impulses may be displaced to people in the immediate environment; then the individual becomes quarrelsome. To some extent blocked interest in life may find expression in sexuality and sociableness. Or assertiveness may be worked off in socially stigmatized ways, like theft and robbery. In contact with representatives of authority, like public relief administrators, personal aggressiveness may increase. The person may justify these acts to himself and to others in the name of collective symbols, like "loyal citizen," "ex-service man who has suffered for his country." Individual acts of terrorism may be justified to "blast a rotten system."

Organized, as distinct from private, activity may be expressed in ceremonials which leave the overt environment unchanged. Persons may associate themselves with sects which spend hours confessing, singing, dancing, listening. Or an organization will sponsor simple and circumscribed demands. Thus committees of the unemployed may protest against "abuses" of power by administrators. Again, there may be elaborate demands for institutional reconstruction, like the socialization of production. And these larger demands may be associated with methods which are conventional, like electioneering and voting, or drastic and forbidden, like general strikes and armed uprisings.

The foregoing alternatives may be expressed in this general form:

> Privately internalized acts
> Privately externalized acts
> Socially internalized acts
> Socially externalized acts.

Political analysis is partly concerned with the discovery of which people act which way under which conditions. Conduct in a given situation can be partially predicted by noticing how those who are involved in it have responded to similar situations in the past, and with what success.

A study of the Chicago unemployed, by Gabriel Almond and the writer, was intended to contribute to our knowledge of *who* responded *how* to the deprivation of unemployment. Who would resort to "privately externalized acts" and who would resort to "socially externalized acts"?

Hyperaggressiveness in face-to-face relations was

found to be an alternative to organized protest. Hyperaggressiveness was discovered by observing the conduct of clients when they came into personal contact with administrators of public relief. A sample of 100 hyperaggressives contrasted in certain respects with a sample of 100 members of protest organizations, like Workers' Committees or Unemployed Councils. The hyperaggressives, unlike the organized, had seldom belonged to parties, unions, or fraternal organizations before the depression; they had changed their jobs more often, and had been more often on private or public relief; they had more often committed impulsive offenses against the law, like assault; they had more often fled from personal responsibilities (deserted their wives, for example).

In general the hyperaggressives were psychopathic personalities who were so narcissistic that they had little love to give to organized activity, so overreactive against the submissive tendencies of their personalities that they resented discipline, so uncontrolled in relation to their impulses that they often clashed with their fellows. They were externalized rage types, capable of organized effort only during the most acute crises. When the organized effort first runs into difficulties, such personalities throw off the bonds of discipline and withdraw into isolation.

Hypersubmissiveness was likewise shown to be an alternative to organized protest. One hundred hypersubmissive clients, in contrast with 100 members of protest organizations, had few predepression affiliations with organizations (and especially few with protest groups). They had seldom committed offenses against the law or the mores; they had held modest jobs; they had come from rural districts in the United States and Europe; they had often been stigmatized by their environment (like the Negroes, objects of race prejudice).

Plainly those were most likely to assert themselves collectively who had been members of trades unions, fraternal societies, and similar associations. This mode of dealing with the world was carried over to the emergency situation as well.

More drastic assertiveness, in the form of membership in revolutionary parties, appealed to those who had been connected with radical parties before, and who had most flagrantly defied the mores. The leaders of the communist-led organizations were recruited from those who committed more impulsive violations of the law than had the leaders of the socialist-led organizations. The socialist leaders revealed a higher incidence of those who had committed crimes of calculation against property. The most radical leaders committed crimes of impulse, like assault rather than "crimes of calculation," like forgery. Such leaders had much in common with the hyperaggressive personalities previously described.

Leaders in unemployed groups came from leaders in the party, business, and social life of the predepression epoch; the rank and file came from the rank and file of predepression organizations. It was apparent that the training, skill, and social connections of the leaders of the radical and the less radical movements were more like one another than they were like the rank and file. The principal bond with the rank and file was the symbol in the name of which the leaders elicited support.

It is important to understand the obsolescence processes of political life. Organizations which fail to "get results" leave some of their members passive; others move over to competing symbols and practices. Comparative investigations seem to show that the ruling elite in any organized movement is less mobile than the rank and file; after all, the rulers are able to extract income, deference, and sometimes safety from their official positions. They build up vested and sentimental bonds to their jobs which are more tangible than those which bind the rank and file. A sampling in 1931 of a branch of the Social Democratic party in mid-Berlin showed that 60 per cent had been members of the party less than five years. Another report on 75,000 members showed that 50 per cent were party members less than five years. Youths, especially, moved from Social Democrat to Communist to National Socialist organizations, and even back again, as recurring waves of success or failure altered their estimate of the total situation. The broad masses are seldom sufficiently active, or sufficiently radicalized, to bind themselves firmly to special means of expression. A self-critical Social Democratic writer showed that, despite generations of proletarian agitation and organization, the proletarian organizations in pre-Nazi Germany exercised a feeble hold on the masses of those who might be called proletarian. Of the forty million proletarians, only 2.5 per cent were to be counted as full members of proletarian parties (Social Democrat, Communist, and fractional Communist parties). Sixty-five per cent of the wage and salaried workers were not in trades unions, and 28 per cent of those who were in trades unions were in "bourgeois unions" (such as those controlled by religious organizations).

The problem of readjustment is plainly connected with the level of general insecurity, which is a function of the way in which environmental changes are interpreted as inflicting indulgences or deprivations. Kautilya's *Arthasastra,* the Indian classic, divides the discontented into the "provoked," "alarmed," "ambitious," and "haughty," and considers the methods which will arouse them against a particular ruler or win them over. The principal contribution of modern analysis is no doubt the discovery of time, and the emphasis upon the processes by which world movements are facilitated or impeded. Plainly the same volume of unemployment may be more dangerous to an elite which is close to the center of the current revolutionary wave than to an elite which is far away. Warsaw is far more menaced than New York.

The focus of discussion so far has been the relationship between person and person, or person and community. The same categories of analysis are relevant to the study of connections of community to community, especially of one state in relation to other states in the modern state system. The sudden defeat of a state may lead to a wave of suicides among its humiliated leaders, and to such internalized collective behavior as religious revivalism. Organized action may also undertake the economic and technical rehabilitation of the nation, for the recovery of status and the exaction of revenge (France after 1870; Germany after 1918).

The same major categories may be used to examine the consequences of contact between persons of contrasting cultures.

The expansion of European civilization has left in its wake a broad wave of cultural crises whose varied outcomes furnish examples of cultural adaptation as well as cultural collapse. An important factor in the outcome is the speed and magnitude of outside interference. But some cultures which have been subject to about the same degree of restriction through contact with Europeans have disintegrated quickly, while others have adapted themselves and survived.

By cultural survival is meant the preservation of the identifying name of the culture and many of its distinctive supporting symbols and practices, and the maintenance of a population to transmit the cultural heritage. Sometimes a smooth and gradual transition is made to effective participation as a member of the body politic of a state which is recognized in the Western European state system. The older tribal name is preserved as a respected social mark, but there are no demands to become a state. No doubt the Maori of New Zealand represent this form of adaptation.

In some instances the carriers of a primitive culture have internalized their behavior to such an extreme degree that the culture moved rapidly toward extinction, not only through the abandonment of its forms, but through the self-destruction of its bearers. W. H. R. Rivers proposed to explain the depopulation of Melanesia on this hypothesis, since he rejected the view that external interference had been more severe here than in areas where the results were less decisive. His interpretation was that the appearance of the white man who violated all sacred restrictions and suffered no harm created such frustration, depression, and lassitude that cultural patterns were neglected, and the people became too uninterested even to procreate.

The same process may occur less spectacularly when many individuals desert a primitive culture, find it impossible to establish a foothold in the larger environment outside, and ultimately destroy themselves by the excessive use of drugs or by the careless contraction of diseases. Those who remain loyal to the primitive culture may adhere strictly to old forms, sometimes failing to adopt enough of the new to make a smooth transition.

Sometimes the amount of socially internalized conduct increases in response to deprivation. New sects may multiply the amount of time and energy spent in dancing, praying, meditating. They may increase the frequency of autistic experiences among the members of the community, thus modifying the norms of the community. There is some evidence that where the peyote cult has made progress among Pueblo Indians, as at Taos, the importance of personal, subjective events has been increased. As Ruth Benedict has shown, the Pueblo Indians are predominantly matter-of-fact. They do not rely upon the dream as a means of personal contact with power, as do the Plains Indians. Those who chew the peyote (dried cactus) report elaborate visions, often in color, and this private autistic experience seems to represent a novel value in Pueblo life.

Socially externalized acts may use for targets not only the world outside the community but also the community itself. We have seen that when aggressive impulses are blocked, the aggression turns back against the targets which are close to the self. There is evidence that this process often appears in the growth of factions among defeated people, especially when they are accustomed to very assertive behavior. M. E. Opler has reported a striking example of this process among the Mescalero Apache. With the destruction of the buffalo herds and the suppression of marauding bands, the Mescalero were thrown into close proximity to one another on the reservation. The peyote cult spread rapidly among them, but in a peculiar form. Here the cult meetings were theaters of acute conflict among rival shamans, each trying to lead the other into the disclosure of his special secrets. Feuds and reprisals grew so bloody that another adjustment became imperative or the Mescalero seemed doomed to mutual extermination.

The symbols which spread among communities in response to deprivation are related to the previous patterns of external expression. The Indians on the plains were devoted to hunting and fighting, in contrast with the Pueblo Indians of the Southwest who were primarily agriculturists when the white man came; and it was among the Plains Indians that the Ghost Dance, which had many antiwhite features, spread most vigorously.

Some symbols organize collective impulses into acts which influence the overt environment. Conspirative uprisings, like the Boxer rebellion in China, may be full of determined hatred of the foreigner; but without the superior technique of the foreigner, failure is sure, unless other circumstances weaken the encroaching civilization. When the bearers of the superior fighting technique are divided among themselves, the pressure is released on peripheral people of simpler technique, who may then emerge from their remote mountains, deserts, and steppes, and sweep in to destroy alien communities or to settle down and become assimilated.

Socially externalized forms of adjustment occur when foreign techniques of agriculture, trade, craftsmanship, manufacturing, and fighting are adopted in the community.

Externalized forms of adjustment may also involve the borrowing of the symbols and the institutional practices of the limiting civilization. Thus nationalistic programs may be borrowed and spread, as the Chinese, for example, are taking over the Western conceptions of the competitive state system and nationalism, and turning them against the Western powers by abolishing extraterritoriality and other kinds of foreign privilege. Among feebler peoples, the precursors of nationalism may appear in the multiplication of native sects in competition with sects and denominations which are foreign controlled. It is reported that among the negro natives of Southwest Africa there are more than 500 native denominations which have been formed in recent years. This is no doubt a cultural activity which tides the negroes through a long period of watchful waiting for the external balance of power to shift to the advantage of the black and against the white.

The foregoing considerations have shown how contact may be met by internalized or externalized acts, some of which give impetus to passive or active programs. What are the factors which affect the geographical distribution of loyalties? Modern nationalistic movements have consolidated the loyalties of the inhabitants of many local areas around symbols of much larger communities. But the reverse has been equally true. The history-less nations of Central and Eastern Europe were stimulated to self-discovery or rediscovery in recent times. The result was to disrupt the continuity of administration in the Austro-Hungarian, Russian, and Turkish empires. Such demands for self-determination in the name of a national unity often follow old administrative lines. Great Britain and France were both organized around urban centers of old administrative districts. The speech of the capital became the standard language of justice, civil and military administration, debate, learning, society. Such unifying traits were often incompletely diffused into outlying provinces. Hence cultural differences could be inflamed into political separatism as national status came to be more highly prized.

Despite the persuasive or the militant pretensions of many self-styled world elites, the world is no unified community. It has no solidarity of sentiment and practice. Such unification has thus far been blocked by the spontaneous and partly deliberate play of the balance of power, or, more correctly, the balancing of power. The play of the balance restricts the scope of an ambitious monarch, an expanding bourgeois state, a militantly revolutionary society. It is the balance of power that has tipped the scales against every local aspirant to world hegemony, and left the nations of mankind loyal to symbols more inclusive than neighborhoods but less inclusive than the world. No external threat, no common hope of gain, no common code of right, has attained the ascendancy which would ensure the peaceful succession of an elite in a united world.

Loyalties may follow functional no less than geographical lines. The new division of labor inaugurated by machines created conspicuous differences between those who toiled in plants and those who owned or managed them. When peasants moved to cities, multifarious insecurities arose. Older codes of morals and manners underwent terrific stress, and found expression in protest symbols directed against the ruling "class." When a revolutionary situation in Russia led to the seizure of power in the name of the "proletariat," processes of geographical restriction got under way at once, as foreign elites sought to protect themselves by emphasizing the parochial characteristics of the new elites. Whether insecurities will be expressed in symbols of geography or of function is largely a matter of their position in time and space with reference to the world-revolutionary process itself.

When are individual impulses displaced upon collective symbols? Periods of prosperity are periods of individualistic expression, when private plans are formed with reference to a benevolent universe. Periods of depression or of war are periods of submission to collective symbols.

When are conciliatory or militant attitudes most likely to be adopted? Cruelty is especially common among those who have felt guilty and inferior, and who seek to overcome submissive tendencies by over-reaction. The externalized rage types and the partially inhibited rage types are those from whom destructive acts are to be expected under stress. Elites and communities which have felt guilty and inferior, and which struggle to overcome lack of self-confidence, are most disposed to orgiastic rage and to acts of collective destruction.

The attitudes which are of particular interest to the student of politics have been passed in terse review: externalized attitudes, community attitudes, militant attitudes, and their correlatives. When we consider these attitudes in the perspective of world development, we cannot fail to be impressed by the tenacity with which certain forms of attitude, included within the pattern of Western European civilization, have persisted in competition and conflict with rival attitudes. This civilization is favorable to externalization, militancy, and parochialism. Energies are directed outward toward the manipulation of man and nature. The expectation of violence leads to the incessant evaluation of social change in terms of fighting effectiveness. Local groups who participate in the technical processes of this civilization are split off from one another by the expectation of violence as a probable resolution of internal and external difficulties, and by the sentimentalizing of local differences. This sentimentalization of local differences has taken the modern form of nationality and nationalism. Nationalism is a mass demand to become or to remain a state among states.[1] Nationalism is a form of provincialism which was stimulated as modern commerce and industry emphasized the advantages of larger markets.

But tendencies to enlarge the local market were checked by conflict with others in the same civilization who were striving for the same extension of market. Tendencies to externalize human activities along profitable economic lines proved incompatible with tendencies to respect localism and to expect resorts to violence. No unified economic group rose to the direction of world-economic processes, since each economic group sought to strengthen its position by emphasizing patriotism and practicing violence, which in turn prevented complete unity with dominant economic groups elsewhere, who were stressing the same things.

Functional symbols rise from time to time to challenge the ascendancy of parochial symbols. The most recent attack on parochialism has been in the name of a world-wide proletarian class. But the other characteristics of Western European civilization have nullified, or are nullifying, the success of these appeals for a functional path to a unified world. Those who seize power in the name of an all-inclusive symbol are promptly isolated by the play of the balance of power, which is particularly sensitive in a civilization that expects violence and sentimentalizes nationality and

[1] For naturalistic as distinguished from certain normative (juristic) purposes, the state may be defined as a manifold of events. "That subjective event which is the unique mark of the state is the recognition that one belongs to a community with a system of paramount claims and expectations." (Quoted from the author's *Psychopathology and Politics*, chapter XIII, "The State as a Manifold of Events," p. 245.)

nationalism. In self-defense, the bearers of the new appeal to functional universality accept the basic conditions of survival in this environment, and emphasize their own local values in a world of potential violence. Hence we are not surprised to learn that the word *Rodina*, meaning birthplace or homeland, is permitted in the press of the Soviet Union in referring to the U.S.S.R. Phrases like "Socialist Fatherland" were formerly used to emphasize the idea of internationalism.

Everywhere the activism, militancy, and parochialism of Western civilization combine to overwhelm all whose attitudes stand opposed.

PART IV: *Résumé*

TEN

RÉSUMÉ

By the study of politics is here meant the study of influence and the influential. The influential cannot be satisfactorily described by the use of a single index. To some extent influence is indicated by claims over values, like deference, income, safety. But deference may not go to the rich, and safety may not go to the distinguished. Plainly different results may be obtained by different criteria of influence.

The results of political analysis depend also on the characteristics of the elite which it is proposed to explore. This book has spoken of skill, class, personality, and attitude groups, and discussed the meaning of social change for the relative ascendancy of such formations. The most important political analysis of modern times (the Marxist) has concentrated attention upon the class results of social change. This has diverted attention from many equally relevant ways of viewing the results of social life, such as the fate of skill, personality, and attitude groups.

Emphasis on class, like emphasis on skill or personality, is a methodological contrivance of systematic thinkers, a selected frame of reference to be held constant during the course of a *particular* act of analysis. The act of using new frames of reference for purposes of political analysis will, as usual, modify the preferences of those who use them. Those accustomed to think in terms of community attitudes (like nationality, nationalism) have often obtained new insights by the use of class analysis, and often modified their practical preferences. Sometimes they have turned from patriotism to proletarianism. Thinkers accustomed to class analysis may be led to new insights and new scales of preference by becoming accustomed to other ways of construing social results. They may want to identify themselves with the skill struggle rather than the class struggle, or to seek fulfillment in the name of nation or race or personality. Any act of analysis chastens preferences by the very act of exposing them to new naturalistic insights.

In communities which share Western European civilization the few, called here the elite, are more influential than the many, the mass. Lord Bryce said that government was always government by the few, whether in the name of the one, the few, or the many.

The ascendancy of an elite depends in part upon the successful manipulation of its environment. Methods of management involve symbols, violence, goods, practices. Counter-elites depend upon the same means.

Some methods are especially adapted to elite attack and others to elite defense. An established elite is usually so well situated in control of the goods, violence, and practices of a community that a challenging elite is constrained to rely chiefly upon symbols. After all, symbols are cheap and elusive; they can be spread by word of mouth beyond the eye of vigilant authority; they can organize concerted action among the disaffected and promote the crisis in which other methods are serviceable. Any established order possesses a dominant myth (ideology); but a symbol monopoly is less easy to protect than a monopoly of goods and violence.

A smoothly functioning political order has little need of thought about propaganda among members of its own community. An ideology, once accepted, perpetuates itself with remarkable vitality. The individuals born into the state direct some of their love toward the symbols which sustain the system: the common name, the common heroes, the common mission, the common demands. Some destructive tendencies are directed against rivals, traitors, heresies, and counterdemands. Individuals generate feelings of guilt in connection with the complex process of growing up; and some of this guilt is projected away from the individual and upon symbols of collective enemies, which are treated as shameful violators of the mores. Personal weakness, too, is projected upon the world outside; after all, is not the enemy destined to defeat in our victory?

The propaganda of revolution has at least one long-run advantage. Discontent, however created, tends to weaken the hold of the dominating system of symbol and practice. Any elite which fails to coincide with prosperity and victory may be rejected by the masses. Defeat, depression, and disaster, however caused, raise doubt about the legitimacy of the Son of Heaven. When individuals are deprived, they tend to withdraw their love from symbols of the external world and to concentrate affection upon themselves; also to divert their assertive impulses from the world outside back against themselves. Extreme reactions result in a narcissistic psychosis, or suicide. Most people, however, avoid such extremes by substituting a new set of collective symbols for the old symbols. The problem of a revolutionary propagandist is to guide miscellaneous insecurities into channels suitable to his seizure of power. He seeks to control the projection of love, destructiveness, guilt, and weakness with reference to a utopia capable of becoming ideology.

Deprivations, alone, are insufficient to produce revolutionary upheavals. Social revolutions occur when new indulgences have been made possible by the growth of new social formations as an incident of technical development. Only the new self-confidence of success gives strength for resentment against deprivation.

It is the recurring surge of insecurity that, however initiated, places a premium upon incessant innovation of detail, both in keeping and in taking power. Boredom with one symbol signifies the importance of another symbol; failure of the army emphasizes the importance of the air force; failure of free competition indicates the possibilities of monopoly; discontent with legislatures suggests the popularity of strong executives.

The harmless discharge of mass emotion (catharsis) can be induced by propaganda, by violence, or by the management of goods and practices. Adjustment, too, can be furthered by each method. But all methods are susceptible to defeat through ineptitude and unpropitious circumstances.

The results of social change are politically significant as they affect the distribution of values among elites of various kinds. Elites have been described here in terms of skill, class, personality, attitude.

Some types of skill have seldom led to eminence. Manual workers, peasants, physical scientists, engineers (manipulators of things) have been far less conspicuous than have managers of men. In Western European civilization, skill in violence, organization, bargaining, and symbol manipulation has been important at all times. But the relative role has varied. Skill in violence was a major way to power in feudal Europe. Skill in organization provided the cement which integrated the national monarchies. Skill in bargaining arose with the age of industrial expansion. In recent crises of world development, skill in propaganda played a decisive role, and skill in bargaining went into partial eclipse.

The growth of new classes, like the growth of new skills, is intertwined with the appearance of new means of production. New technology was a major precondition of the decline of aristocracy and the rise of the bourgeoisie. This was in part signalized by the seizure of power in France (and elsewhere) during crises of great intensity. A world revolution is a seizure of power which benefits a new social formation. This seizure is local, and proceeds in the name of a new set of ruling symbols. The French Revolution, it will be remembered, was carried out in the name of the "rights of man," and some of the practices were universal suffrage, parliamentarism, church disestablishment, and the encouragement of businessmen at the expense of feudal aristocrats.

We have accepted the proposition that the revolution of 1917 in Russia was another world revolution. Those who seized power spoke in the name of the proletariat, and instituted relative equality of money incomes, governmentalization of organized social life, monopolization of legality in the hands of a single dominant party. Where do we stand with reference to this latest revolutionary upheaval and the next one?

Our analysis has drawn attention to the way that world-revolutionary initiatives are at once partially restricted and partially universalized. Those who seized power in France and Russia were restricted by the play of the external balance of power. Hence the world was not united by those who spoke in the name of the new political symbols. One of the means of defense was partial incorporation of symbols and practices connected with this pattern. Thus we interpret the present juncture of world affairs as a movement toward relative money equality, toward governmentalization of social life, and toward the monopoly of legality by single political parties.

From this point of view we are in the midst of a unified world movement which is expressing itself in many contradictory forms during its early phases. In the United States it is doubtful if these developments will pass through a period of *"romantic"* Fascism, as in Italy and Germany. Romantic Fascism is marked by a seizure of offices behind a tenuous façade of legality by leaders of a mass movement. The backbone of the popular movement is the lower middle class; the agitators at the top receive support from big business and aristocratic groups as well. At first private capitalism is conserved; but it seems probable that in the face of the necessity for a united nation, private capitalism will be liquidated in times of military stress. In a military state, the movement toward equalization, governmentalization, and monopolization would no doubt proceed.

Another possible path to Fascism in the United States would involve the steady encroachment of an impatient community upon the use of the strike. This *"piecemeal"* Fascism could come about as middle-class groups are aroused against the "agitators," "reds," and "radicals" by organized agencies of big business and big finance.

A more peaceful development of American life might follow were the middle classes emancipated from their present psychological dependence upon the agencies of big business and big finance. At present spokesmen of nationwide organizations of businessmen speak in the name of American business as a unit, without emphasizing the conflict of interest between independent business and monopolistic business. In the past the discontent of independent business and professional groups at the monopoly tendencies of modern industrialism has been exhausted through partisan channels. Effective action in the modern world depends upon functional organizations which lie behind parties and which confer strength upon partisan action. Hence the growth of middle-class consciousness depends upon organizing middle-class groups into effective national bodies which command their own executive staffs, their own means of communication, and which develop their own self-consciousness, outlook, and program.

As far as the United States is concerned, the organization of an Independent Chamber of American Business and Service would foster middle-class activism. Practical demands could be made to use the taxing power to curb big business and big finance, and to provide credit to independent groups. On this program, the smaller business and professional man can cooperate, within limits, with the organizations of labor, especially skilled labor. The smaller agricultural interests can be closely identified with antimonopoly demands. These several components of the middle class might be united for common purposes in an American Skill Congress, welcoming all Americans who have sacrificed to obtain socially useful skill, and who belong to the lesser-income group. In annual assembly, the American Skill Congress could coordinate the scattered programs of cooperating organizations and stimulate effective skill consciousness among them.

Such a capstone agency would stimulate effective self-consciousness among social formations which are now driven hither and yon by historical processes into which they have little insight. Perhaps the supreme paradox is that it is precisely the skill groups of the lower middle classes which are rising to control in modern world politics. In the Soviet Union present developments favor those who get skill in engineering, organization, propaganda, violence. Vast differences in money income were wiped out with the extinction of the landed aristocracy and hierarchies of private business. In the United States, where middle-class formations are still relatively flourishing, world developments to curb great differences of income may take somewhat distinctive form.

Recently independent druggists, hardware dealers, grocers, and other businessmen have undertaken to curb the chain stores. They have been supported by wholesalers who were alarmed by the possibility that their own markets would be dominated by the chains. Some small manufacturing concerns are run by men who are alert to the possible advantages to be derived from protecting their independence through organized action. The canning industry, widely dispersed over the nation in many small units, is typical of the most promising bases of middle-class politics. Many businessmen were stimulated to greater awareness of their special interests when they saw their large competitors seek to monopolize the machinery of the National Industrial Recovery Act. Some have seen the advantages to be gained by them from cheap power furnished by such government enterprises as the Tennessee Valley Authority, the Boulder Dam, and the Grand Coulée project. A government "yardstick" can be used to control the rates of private utility companies.

It has recently been perceived that the devices of modern corporate control may be used as instruments of public, as well as private, policy. Large private utility companies, notably in the fields of power and communication, have spread their stock widely throughout the nation. It was hoped that the vested interests thus created would protect the utilities against demands for public ownership and operation. At the same time it was believed that the nominal owners were too widely dispersed to exercise any degree of effective influence over the small controlling groups which dominated the holding operating companies.

Public policy may require the use of "shares" not only to propagate the illusion of control as a "public relations policy," but to provide the means of efficient control. Governments have already learned to use the publicly owned corporation, and there are many instances of joint subscription of share capital by public authority and private groups and individuals. An infinitely large variety of joint arrangements is conceivable. Important credit, power, transportation, and communication enterprises (regional, national, extra-national) could have voting shares assigned to significant functional groups, like Federal government departments and commissions, business associations (including dependents), farmers, organized workers, consumers, cooperatives, state and metropolitan governments.

At present it is common, as a public relations policy, to assign blocs of stock to a "preferred list" of individuals who are connected with banks, brokerage houses, investment trusts, insurance companies, engineering companies, and political parties. This practice can be "institutionalized" and brought under more responsible control by assigning shares to important functional groups in their corporate capacities.

If this, or any other, control device is set up, the results will depend upon the relative skill and strength of functional groups. If middle-income skill groups are to influence national policy in their own behalf, they must be nationally organized, capable of independent self-assertion. They must be represented by a set of spokesmen who will not be misled by the spokesmen of some big business groups who complain of "reds" when independent business, professional, and labor groups threaten to curb monopolistic practices.

Imaginative minds have already forecast the day when devices of corporate control would be adapted to the requirements of integrated national policy. They have foreseen the possibility of "every citizen a shareholder" in "U.S.A., Incorporated," enjoying a guaranteed basic income as a fixed charge on the national economic enterprise (contingent upon satisfactory participation in the national undertaking), and belonging to functional-territorial groups capable of exercising some formal, rather than clandestine or external, influence over policy.

Entirely apart from such ambitious projects are many less pretentious devices for coping with the "efficiency and acceptability" problems of large-scale undertakings in the American Republic. Many ingenious practices are proposed in the works of such seasoned students of modern society as Sidney and Beatrice Webb.

Some men of substantial property will see that the preservation of American business depends upon a healthy middle class of business and professional Americans. Big business needs smaller business, and can wisely adopt measures necessary to sustain it. Otherwise the cleavage between rich and poor, so disastrous for the preservation of republican institutions, will widen to alarming proportions. *The Federalist* faced these issues with the utmost candor during the critical days of debate on the adoption of the new Constitution. Plainly, "the most common and durable source of factions has been the various and unequal distribution of property." It was taken for granted that factions could not be eliminated, but that their effects could be controlled. And there were some among the early statesmen of the United States who saw that something might be done to preserve that considerable dispersion of economic control upon which the stability of republican government depends.

While the literature of class analysis is abundant, the meaning of social life for the relative success of personality types has been but little explored. Yet the ebb and flow of events favors now one, now another, style of personality. The principal trait of the politician, in general, is intense craving for deference; but this motive must be joined with appropriate skills and with propitious circumstances if success is to come. Within the general pattern of the politician several subtypes are discernible. Notable is the agitator, whose urge for deference is so intense that he is content with

nothing less than the *excited* response of his contemporaries. As means to excitement he cultivates the
skills of oratory and polemical journalism. The organizer is less bound to the need for excited response;
he has more energy for coordinating human activity.
Conciliatory personalities come from the partly inhibited rage types; ruthless and imperious personalities, from externalized rage types. Agitational and
ruthless types are both favored by crisis, and they have
been abundantly in evidence during the recent crises
of world economic expansion-contraction. Organizers
and conciliatory personalities are more favored by the
periods between crises, and by the initial phases of
stress.

Social developments may be seen with reference to
their effect upon attitude groups. Though closely related to other frames of reference, attitude groups cut
across all of them. The most diverse personality types
may share the same nationalistic loyalty; the most
similar personality types may be separated by class
loyalties. Men whose skill is violence may be very
group-conscious and politically assertive; men whose
skill is engineering are notably less active in politics.
The success of classes may be impeded by attitudes of
national loyalty.

The civilization of Western Europe is distinguished
by certain attitudes which survive the most varied
local developments, and impose themselves upon successive generations. European civilization is activistic:
it fosters the manipulation of man and nature; it favors
the externalizing rather than the internalizing of human impulses. European civilization is parochial: it
fosters local loyalties, like nationalism, and curbs the
tendency to assert functional loyalties as a means of
universal union. European civilization has the expectation of violence; it takes wars, revolutions, secessions,
revolts, gang struggles, and homicide for granted;
regardless of how violence may be deplored, the probability of violence is sorrowfully assumed by the over-

whelming majority. There are other cultures ("primitive" cultures) which take none of these things for granted. But the Western European pattern now holds most of mankind in its clutches.

Perhaps the distinguishing and unifying political movement of our times is the emergence of the lesser-income skill groups to hegemony in a world where the partial diffusion, partial restriction of the world-revolutionary pattern of 1917 is taking place atop the world created by the revolution of 1789. Yet behind the grandeur of class façades a penetrating political analysis can disclose the additional, perhaps subtler, dialectics of personal skills, personality types, personal attitudes. Thus the study of politics can lead to no once-for-all accomplishment, no gratifying certainty; it can give some measure of orientation for the incessant reappraisal of the shifting lines of communal insecurity.

PART V: *Postscript*

ELEVEN

POSTSCRIPT (1958)

When you have been away from an American town for a while and ask what has happened in politics you are told who has been elected to what office, or appointed to which job. It will not be hard to discover whose political star is rising or falling, and who is working with or against whom. Jones, it appears, has broken with Smith and run against him in the last election. Smith, we are told, alienated the Negro vote on the school issue, and lost trades union support by his stand when the municipal employees struck. We may hear that Jones now has the support of the State Democratic machine, and has a good chance for the Governorship. Smith has strong friends in Washington and rumor says that he will soon be taken care of with a Federal job. And so on and on.

Now is this what politics is about? If so we may very well ask why anybody bothers to study the subject. Any well-informed journalist, lobbyist, interest group representative, or lawyer would seem to know all there is to know; and besides, he keeps up to date.

The same question can be raised about business. If you want to know what has been happening find a business acquaintance or a business reporter and ask him. He can summarize which stocks have been going up or down, which firms have been expanding or shrinking, and who is now on the list of richest men or women. Is there any point to studying economics when such information is readily at hand?

If we are in a question raising mood skepticism may extend to every other sphere of social life. Take churches, for example. It is possible to find an individual who is informed about changes in the number of churches and in their membership, and who can say which clergymen have become more or less popular as public personalities.

Or take educational institutions. We can learn who holds top administrative posts in the colleges, high schools, grade schools and vocational schools of the region. Information is available about number of students and trends in the level of excellence in mathematics, the sciences, and other subjects of examination.

Consider such agencies of public enlightenment as radio-TV, newspapers, magazines and books. We can quickly identify the most important publishers and station owners, and the best known commentators. Regular readers or viewers will report whether there has been a change in the amount of space or time spent on civic affairs.

If we ask about family life we may be told that the Hills section is full of broken homes, and of neighborhood quarrels. On the other hand certain new districts are said to be full of congenial people who like to do things together.

Congeniality may be closely connected with the social acceptability of an area. The persons in the Hills section, for instance, were once among the most respected elements of the community. But families of social prestige, we are told, have moved out. We may learn in fact that top-drawer families have moved outside the city limits.

We may hear a great deal about the state of safety, health and comfort during recent times. New traffic systems have cut down the accident rate. Better alarm systems are credited with having reduced burglaries and other crimes. New hospitals have become available; and many long standing nuisances, like loud factory whistles, smoke and open garbage dumps, have disappeared.

As our information begins to catch up with events in the community our questions about government and politics take on a different character. Instead of asking about individual careers we begin to inquire about the role government has played in connection with the changes that have been going on throughout the entire community.

Consider business, for instance. We are asking to what extent the bonding authority of the municipality has been used to obtain the capital necessary to install an airport, to relocate freight and passenger terminals, to clear new industrial districts. Or churches. Has the planning authority of the city been used to make strategic sites available to churches in all the communities that have developed around the new shopping service centers? Educational institutions. Of the total amount of money that goes into education at every level (and for every professional, occupational and artistic skill) how much has been raised by government? (Local? State? National?) Think of the media of public enlightenment. Has the government channel of action been used to establish radio-TV stations in order to break up a private monopoly? And to encourage further diversity by encouraging independent or competing services to come into the locality? Consider family and neighborhood life. Has the government been alert enough to arrest the disintegration of residential neighborhoods by using its planning authority to give protection against non-residential encroachments? And to make sites available for community facilities needed for a constructive common life? Are governmental authorities awake to the challenge of "upgrading" socially disrespected groups by the use of residential building and neighborhood development projects? Has the government been effectively employed to take the initiatives required to cut down accidents, disease, physical violence, and public nuisances?

To raise such questions is to bring into the open the need of a more comprehensive picture of government and politics than can come from casual interviewing and reading. A map of public affairs is required that is carefully researched and systematically organized. Obviously the preparation of such a map is beyond the professional duty of a city councilman or a newspaper editor. Hence we are brought to the professional student of government, the political scientist. It is his special task to provide a comprehensive account of what governments are doing. This implies that he must go far beyond the limits of one city or county. If the significance of local trends is to be grasped it must be seen in the perspective of the region and the nation; and some important points will appear when the national picture is supplemented with information about trends in Canada and other nations whose tradition is predominantly English. We also share many historic and contemporary traits and interests with the peoples of Western Europe; and the years are gradually bringing us into closer contact with the new nations of the world.

We depend upon specialized students of government to hold mirrors up to the government and politics of any locality. One mirror is statewide or regional; another is sectional or national; another is continental, or hemispherical, or oceanic (e.g., the

Atlantic, the Pacific). It may be a traditional area with many cultural characteristics in common (the English-speaking peoples), a major bloc in world politics (the Soviet world), or the world as a whole.

It is quite impossible to examine phenomena of such range, interest and practicality without raising a host of questions. A basic issue is the effect of relying exclusively upon the channel of government to carry out a given social activity; or of leaving the matter almost entirely to private initiatives, or of striking a balance at a point between. Assuming that some activities are to be within the province of government many problems of organization appear. How centralized shall the organization be (internationally, nationally, regionally, locally)? At any "horizontal" level, like the metropolitan district, how concentrated shall the top decisions be (in one organ? two or more co-ordinate organs)? In regard to the decisions taken at any level how active shall the electorate (with what qualifications) be?

Even this abbreviated list is enough to remind the informed reader of scores of issues that relate to the organization of government at every level. Such questions are the professional stock in trade of scholars who variously describe themselves as specialists on comparative government, public administration, and public law.

Most of the problems mentioned deal directly with the "structure" of government; and we have implied that the expert who contributes to their solution is a student of "government." This usage is unobjectionable provided that it is not assumed to imply that the expert limits his study to the organized details of official agencies. We believe that no important conclusion can be reached that does not rest upon a wider basis of knowledge than the structural details of government agencies.

The Contextual Approach

The fundamental importance of the contextual requirement can be recognized if, for instance, we refresh our memories about some facts of municipal government. I refer to the mode of apportioning a city council. In the city government of the United States during the nineteenth century the prestige of the Federal Constitution was such that cities fashioned themselves in the image of Federal systems. City legislatures were often split into two chambers; and councillors were chosen from territorial constituencies (wards). Because corruption became rampant in city government the tendency has been to repudiate both "bicameralism" and wards. Even professional students of government not infrequently assume that local legislatures, when elected by districts, are predestined to corruption. It is possible to show that such an assertion is false. English municipalities were relatively free of corruption at the time American cities were brimming with bribery and favoritism; and English councils were chosen by ward. An explanation might be that the people who went into city government in England, or who kept watch on local affairs, made different demands upon government and upon themselves in relation to government than their opposite numbers in America. Interviews with knowledgeable persons would, in all probability, quickly confirm this hypothesis.

Studies that give attention to the context in which formal structures of government operate are often called studies of "politics" rather than "government." This distinction is not only vague; it has created confusion by using two words ("government," "politics") to cover the same frame of reference. In the present discussion we use the term "politics" as the global word, leaving "government" free to receive a more specialized meaning. The important point, however, is not to standardize the term but to underscore the point that, irrespective of terms, no detail of governmental organization can be fully understood apart from its relationship to the context of which it is part. This is the contextual principle (or, synonymously, the configurative principle) of politics.

Five Key Questions

It becomes apparent, as we have seen in connection with our initial allusions to city affairs, that five questions are pertinent to every political situation:

What goal values are to be sought?
What are the trends in the realization of values?
What factors condition trends?
What projections characterize the probable course of future developments?
What policy alternatives will bring the greatest net realization of values?

Goals. The first question is the traditional problem of political philosophy.

Trends. The second suggests the special task of political and social history.

Conditions. The third is the scientific question. It calls for the systematic statement of theory and the use of empirical methods of gathering and processing data.

Projections. The projecting of future lines of political change is less commonly cultivated as a systematic intellectual task than the others—and this, despite the fact that all decisions depend upon assumptions about the future.

Alternatives. Students of politics are expected to have something pertinent to offer about the probable effects of adopting one form of government or another, or one policy or another relating to power.

Although the five questions apply to any problem in politics we recognize that particular specialists concern themselves with each one. Philosophers and theologians are, as was said, traditionally assumed to have something clarifying to say about values. It is assumed that historians will slowly piece out the story of past relations between aspiration and achievement. But historians are not the only contributors. Since non-literate societies of American Indians, Pacific Islanders and Afro-Asians must be described by other methods than those traditionally employed by historians, social anthropologists have come into being to fill in the world picture of trend.

Although much of their energy goes into time sequences this is not the chief aim of anthropologists. In common with sociologists, economists and political scientists they think of themselves as scientists; hence they are responsible for *explaining* the phenomena which engage their professional interest. It would be mistaken to assume that all scholars who call themselves historians are uninterested in improving our theoretical knowledge of social change. But there is no doubt that great disparity exists between the relative emphasis of historians on the one hand and of political scientists (or other social disciplines) on the other. A scientist keeps theory at the center of attention; historians think first about the sequence and spread of events in time and space.

Historians and social scientists recognize that connections between past and future exist in the sense that some predictions can validly be made if past trends and conditions are faithfully described. If we look at the flow of events in one city we can anticipate some sequences of upcoming events. We can, for instance, foretell that administrative and legislative districts will be readjusted to conform to population shifts. If we widen the survey to include an entire State, our image of the future may be modified. We may see that counter-trends are gathering strength; it may appear therefore that the bulge in city *A's* population is a flash in the pan resulting from an industry nearing the end of a great boom. Many other predictions may be revised as the map is widened and local occurrences are viewed in larger perspective. We may in fact come to the provisional conclusion that a wide belt of populated centers is likely to be evacuated and turned into a buffer zone of radioactive contamination as a measure of military security.

It is essential to emphasize the crucial significance of the task of estimating the future as part of the process of making decisions. A decision is necessarily a step into the future. The inference is that one way to improve the rationality of decision is by improving these estimates. It is generally recognized that public officials and typical members of an electorate are too busy with affairs of the moment to devote much attention to the difficult intellectual task of challenging current conceptions of the future. Thus votes are continually being cast for or against military appropriations, or economic and cultural aid, or more effective international governmental organization, with a minimum of critique of fundamental expectations. I believe that a major responsibility of the specialist on politics is to re-edit maps of the future, and to improve the methods by which the job is done.

It is generally held that the evaluation of policy alternatives is more a field of professional competence than that of the making of comprehensive estimates of the future. A specialist can make himself comfortable among alternatives of policy by the expedient device of adopting successive sets of working assumptions about future contingencies. The expert can in this way evade the responsibility for committing himself to a definite estimate of the likelihood that a given contingency will in fact appear. In this way the expert keeps his statements about the future in the form of disguised repetitions of observations and analyses of the past.

Fostering "Breakthroughs" in History

Why do we place so much emphasis upon that part of the thinker's task which consists in noting the formation of trends and of formulating developmental constructs of the future? The general answer is that these intellectual operations are capable of contributing, to remarkable degree, to the "breakthroughs" that occur in the decision processes of history.

It would be wise to examine it in more detail, since this proposition is far from receiving universal support. It is possible for everyone to recall a few outstanding occasions on which one person, or a small number of persons, has been able to intervene effectively in the historical process. A striking instance was the act of persuading President Franklin D. Roosevelt to take the chance of financing research and development that led to the atomic bomb. Further, we recall the historical impact of individuals who have broken through accepted political ideologies and, for better or worse, provoked new orientations on a gigantic scale. One thinks immediately of Rousseau and the ideology of democracy; of Marx and the ideology of socialism; of Hitler and the ideology of racism.

When I recommend the "problem of identifying a problem" as a distinctive field of activity for political thinkers am I advocating the initiation of doctrinaire movements? Is the supreme challenge of configurative thinking to "design the next Marxism" or to "give the world a new religion"?

The answer is again in the negative. We accept the difference of function that separates the "thinker-scholar" from the man-of-action. Attempts to combine both do injury, at least to the intellectual function. Dogmatism about the future, for example, is not an attitude appropriate to the "thinker-scholar," however expedient it may be for the political leader, who caters to the craving of dependent and confused personalities, to be imposed upon.

The position taken here is not inconsistent with admitting that work of intellectual distinction can become entangled in an undergrowth of dogmatic delusion (as with Marx), or that the one who successfully plays an inventive intellectual role can also assume some active political roles as well. The active participations that do least damage to intellectual contributions, or that motivate or inform them, are not agitational roles. Former activists often have much of importance to say, as we recognize in the famous example of Machiavelli. Diplomatic, advisory, ministerial and legal posts have often provided a vantage point of political sophistication for creative minds. Almost at random we can recall Hume, Locke and Bodin. It is also possible to name serious contributors to political thought whose lives were spent outside the arena of effective politics, though they have yearned for activity. In this connection we think of the peculiarly unsuccessful initiatives of Confucius, Plato and Hobbes. In the United States some of the greatest contributions to political thinking were "occasional pieces" written by active public men like Jefferson, Madison and Hamilton, and some Justices of the Supreme Court. It is not to be forgotten, however, that key problems have been defined by withdrawn thinkers like Spinoza and rather aloof academic specialists like Pareto and Mosca.

Further Confirmation of the Configurative Principle

It may not be irrelevant to remark in passing that the impressive variety of circumstances in which significant political thought has arisen is a further confirmation of the contextual principle. If we regard the appearance of a significant result as the "constant," it is evident that many "factor combinations" have successfully substituted for one another in bringing it about.

A further verification of the contextual principle is the range of often contradictory detail with which a specific political doctrine, formula or operation has been associated historically in the contemporary world. Does anyone need to be more than reminded that religions and philosophies which celebrate the dignity of man have been used to justify slavery and injustice as well as to promote emancipation and equality? Or that many written constitutions deliberately exploit the symbolism of democracy on behalf of autocratic regimes? As Karl Lowenstein puts it, the "semantic" constitution places no limits whatever upon the power-holding elite, whether one has in mind an individual ruler, a junta, a committee, an assembly or a party. The sovereignty of the people may be unhesitatingly affirmed and popular elections may be provided for. But in the most flagrant cases the face of the document betrays the situation that field research will confirm by the clauses which prescribe that the president can perpetuate himself in office, that elections are conducted on the single-party ticket (and so on). In other bodies politic the manifest content of the constitution may not divulge the effective situation so plainly. Only field work conducted by proper methods will unveil the working of a complex system of indirect election, for example.

Some corollaries of the contextual principle: Any political symbol or practice can be—and probably has been—part of contradictory political patterns. Connections between the details of a political configuration are conditioned by their relationship to the whole rather than by the peculiar characteristics of the details themselves. It is possible to account for the occurrence of similar outcomes in different situations by taking note of diverse, though equivalent, combinations of variables. Similar variables, overwhelmed by the peculiarities of the larger context in which they occur, can be associated with highly contrasting results.

Is the meaning of this that all political events are entirely at random; hence such a detail as taking thought has no effect upon anything else and no possibility of arriving at descriptive truth about anything? The answer, again, is negative. What holds true over long periods of time and in a huge aggregation of contexts may not be true over shorter periods or in lesser areas. If it is true that in the long run all events move toward randomness, it can also be true that events move without randomness over the "runs" which have most immediate concern for us. The "inevitability of randomness" cannot be demonstrated for the unfolding dimensions of future events.

The Creative Significance of Perceiving and Naming

The principal implication of the configurative principle for the political thinker is that the act of perceiving and naming a social pattern can effect both the relationship named and other relations in the context.

Turning points in political thinking, for example, have been the act of articulating key symbols of identity which have facilitated the mutual discovery and active cooperation of men and women of various "nations," "religions," "parties," "industries" or "corporations."

Further, new symbols of demand have labeled some events as desirable culminations of human activity. The demand may be as "tangible" as higher wages or as "intangible" as national honor in a controversy whose details are highly ambiguous and controversial.

Also, new symbols of expectation, such as the destructiveness of atomic weapons or the supposed inevitability of a particular pattern of world revolution, may become relevant.

The conclusion is that a major task for political thinkers in breaking through current stereotypes is to give systematic consideration to all possible "identities" at the local, national and world political level; to inventory all imaginable demands relating to preferred events (values) at all levels; and to assess all conceivable expectations (matter of fact images of past-present-future). When such symbols are brought into the focus of attention of participants in the process of any body politic they are likely to release the energies of motivation and provide guidance for discharge against targets of tension.

These symbol-discoveries may or may not conform to the preferences of the political thinker himself. The exploration of his preferences is not to be excluded. Quite the contrary! We regard such exploration as an obligation. But it is not an exclusive obligation. As a contributor to enlightenment as well as rectitude the political thinker is a physiologist as well as a physician. It is his function to use the resources of the mind to reveal the process of politics in its entirety as well as to shepherd policies toward end-values that appeal to him.

In Quest of Identity

One way to formulate the "trend-discovering" function that may be performed by political thinkers is to conceive of it as a quest for identity. All men who loosen the bonds of the culture into which they are born by becoming aware of it face the eventual challenge of equipping themselves with identity cards. Am I to conceive of myself as a Republican or a Democrat? A Communist or a Socialist? An American or a Cosmopolitan? And so on through a vast array of potential "selves." Are these components of the "self" with which I am deeply involved, or are they worn lightly, to be removed at convenience? Who invented all these rival self-symbols? Who am I? Or rather, as whom shall I identify myself? And what are the implications for the remaining years of life?

The thinker who brings into the focus of full waking awareness symbols that identify selves long lost in history—like Robert Graves, for example—is actively participating in the current re-definition of the self-systems that bind men together or drive them apart. In the same way the thinker who discerns a set of current trends in activity or outlook and draws it more explicitly into general attention is widening the range of freedom of identification which is one of the most fundamental freedoms of any man.

The philosopher and psychologist George Herbert Mead was one of the minds most creatively absorbed in examining the remarkable process by which babies become human beings. Mead drew attention to many fundamental mechanisms in the baby-family constellation that help to illuminate the sequence. Not the least important mechanism is social imitation or "playing the role of the other." In this way the inner lives of the people around us gradually gain intelligibility. Empathy enlarges a person's perception of the subjective events whose focal position is the "consciousness" by an "other" of himself. By playing this role in imagination an individual comes to enlarge the primitive ego symbol and to include with it the symbols of other egos to constitute a self.

Mead quite properly spoke of "playing" the role of the other and described the function of this kind of play in the growth of self-systems. In later phases of the career line the peculiar balance of "reality-fantasy" that characterizes the child's preoccupation with play tends to disappear. Reality references are structured and tested; and the mature participant in society is more distinguished by deliberate "work" than by spontaneous play. The political thinker who draws attention to the collective images that appear to be rising or falling as one secedes from the past into the future is performing for adults the function that every child was once mainly engaged in looking after for himself. The function is the quest of human identity.

The Skill Construct

The inclusive conception of political thought as configurative was given preliminary statement in the first chapter of a book published in 1935, *World Politics and Personal Insecurity*. The *Politics* was published a year later and was intended to highlight selected aspects of the larger conception. Of greatest interest to me was the presentation of various symbols with which human beings can identify in the multifarious situations of contemporary and developing life. Far too much vested and sentimental interest has grown up around identifications such as "nation" or "class." Whole categories of human pluri-potentiality are ignored; the *Politics* presented some different modes of thought.

Attention was drawn to a view of politics in which the chosen frame of reference is the rise and fall of one set of social formations, namely, skill groups. In later publications selected categories of skill groupings have been used to provide relatively new perspectives for the review of historical trends and future developments. One construct took account of the decline of skills of violence (military, police) while industrialism and capitalism spread during the nineteenth century, giving prominence as they rose to the specialized skills of business, of mass political party organization and propaganda; and giving ground in the twentieth century to a renewed wave of specialists on violence as world crises continue.

It is to be expected that the spread of the techno-scientific revolution will favor the further rise in influence of persons skilled in mathematics, physics, and chemistry. Circumstances will become even more propitious for the appearance within the decision process of levels of competence much higher than hitherto in mathematics, logic and science. The competence may of course be acquired during early life and kept intact until one passes into research administration, or into the role of an interest representative for a professional group, an industry or an administrative agency. Barring disaster the chances of the non-skilled (through poor education or incapacity) are much poorer than in the past. Non-skilled work is vanishing as automation retrains personnel to guide and maintain machine installations.

The Class Form of the Skill Construct

The *Politics* also referred to "classes," or large social aggregates of similar function and outlook. The suggestion was made that the skill groups as a whole were superseding traditional formations like landed aristocracies, privileged plutocracies, and manual toilers (true proletarians). Since the *Politics* it has become more apparent in industrialized countries like the United States that maintenance of high levels of business activity depends not only upon high levels of capital investment and productive employment, but upon effective demand widely distributed through the community at large, and capable of moving the goods and services produced by a fabulously productive technology. This has meant a graduated scale of income distribution instead of a pattern in which a very few receivers are widely set apart from others. In such an industrial society political perspectives include both the expectation and demand that effective living standards continue to go up, and that it is within the capacity and therefore is an obligation of government to take whatever measures will prevent or terminate other than temporary recessions.

In some countries the techno-scientific revolution has occurred in a context which fosters a struggle to keep important aspects of the skill revolution in check. Where capital accumulation for industrializing purposes has been forced, and where there has been continuous fear of external interference, ruling elements have felt constrained to prevent the fact that the population is being transformed into a complex tissue of skill groups from undermining obedience to the regime and from compelling the adoption of policies that provide more immediate material gratification.

Invention, Diffusion and Restriction
of Ideological Systems

Politics also considered the rise and fall of groups that cut through the class lines of a given culture, or include less than a whole class formation. The allusion is to "attitude" groups, and particularly to ideological formations accepting or rejecting the patterns in the name of which the Moscow Revolution of late 1917 was carried out. Up to the present moment the world revolutionary radicalism of the original revolutionary elite and its successors has failed to achieve universality. An examination of the sequence shows how several ideologies are related to one another, and also reveals some of the mechanisms by which ideologies rise, diffuse or become restricted in the arena of world politics.

The most apparent fact is the stress that has been put upon "national" symbols of identification as means of restricting the spread of the elites invoking the symbol-system launched in 1917. Even where "communism" is accepted "international communism" may be rejected. Other examples of restriction by partial incorporation (and partial rejection) have occurred among ideological groups which affirm "socialism" yet reject "international socialism" on behalf of autonomous national versions. A parallel process can be detected in the "capitalist" world where a frequent target is "international capitalism" or the "imperialist capitalism" of a strong financial and industrial economy like that of the United States. "National" capitalist movements take the form of demands for economic protectionism by the use of tariffs, import restrictions, currency regulation, business ownership requirements, and subsidies to chosen industries.

Another symbol-pattern cuts across the self-designated believers in communism, socialism or capitalism, whether international or national. It is indicated by the pairing of opposite conceptions like "democracy" versus "despotism" (or, synonymously, "freedom" versus "monopoly," "autocracy," and the like). From the point of view of political semantics "democratic capitalists, socialists, and communists" can line up against "despotic capitalists, socialists and communists." Such a symbolism as "people's capitalism" is a straw in the wind, especially if a coalition forms of those who support "people's capitalism," "people's socialism," and "people's communism" to defeat "despotic capitalists, socialists and communists."

The Racist Case

It is important to keep in mind the vigor with which racist distinctions were supported in Germany and elsewhere in recent years. The racist symbol of identification invoked by the Nazis was a "functional" restriction of all rival ideologies. A restriction is functional when it opposes a new symbol to the distinctive symbols put forward by former ideologies. The French Revolution emphasized legal and political language. The Russian revolution put the accent on economics. Hitler's movement not only retained the economic connotation of "socialism," and the political overtones of "freedom," "party" and "nation," but added "Volk" ("Racist").

The defeat of the Nazis brought about a stunning reversal of this new ideology. But it would be a mistake to assume that it is dead. The expansion of modern science and technology is emphasizing the "non-psychological" characteristics of man and progressively assimilating him to machines. Modern electronics has brought the computer into existence and begun to simulate the brain. Meanwhile, advances in pharmacology have created industries that multiply chemical means of influencing subjective events. Millions of people now modify their moods and drives by the use of other agents than the classical list: tobacco, tea, cocoa, alcohol, opium. Robots are in the making that approach the functions characteristic of living organisms and surpass man in many respects. Experimental embryology, too, is taking means of laying the basis for new forms of life which may exceed the capabilities of the human species.

An ideology appropriate to these developments was stated by Julian Huxley, among others, when he declared that man is taking evolution into his own hands. But the conspicuous role of physical factors in the "Brave New World" of Aldous Huxley creates a situation favorable to "racism" and "machine-ism."

The Personality Construct

It is no longer fanciful to assert that ruling groups can eventually call new battalions of "machine men" and new forms of life into being; or that the era of astropolitics is close by. One of the consequences is to put a new exponent of importance upon the fourth category of social forms mentioned in *Politics*, namely, the forms of personality. Man is on the eve of creating life in his own image, following Divine precedent, or in the image of his aspirations, which is more appropriate in view of his limitations. But which man or men will give decisive direction to the choice of the new forms? A comprehensive conception of drives and mechanisms is called for; and the ideological systems of mankind are applied in relatively different ways according to the basic structures of personality which invoke them. The configurative principle finds one of its most enduring exemplifications in this fundamental intersection. If we design "super men" shall we plan for super-kindliness and eliminate the recurring difficulties built into the gene bank of the human species by our rapacious ancestry?

Outcome Analysis

Although one may say that the most important sections of the *Politics* were focused upon the "who," dealing with key symbols of identity, including their past and future prospects, it would be inaccurate to conclude that other features of political thought were wholly de-emphasized. *Politics* dealt to some extent with the "what" as well as the "who" of the political process.

In characterizing the relative influence of various groups *Politics* spoke broadly of "safety, income and deference." When this branch of political analysis is given more formal treatment the relation of these terms to the value context as a whole is set forth. It is commonplace that living forms pursue outcomes that gratify what are variously referred to as "wants" "drives" "wishes" "predispositions" or "demands" of the individual concerned. We refer to any outcome of the kind as a value (preferred event). All the outcomes sought are not consciously pursued or recognized, although they may come acutely to the focus of attention in situations of conflict.

If we were to make an inventory of all the specific outcomes sought by typical individuals in a given social setting the list would soon run into thousands. We would take note of preferred clothing, food, automobiles, books, houses, pets—and on and on. Lists of the kind are unwieldy unless classified by a few key terms; and this is the function of the eight terms which my colleagues and I have found convenient to standardize for our use since *Politics*. The terms are employed to classify all the value outcomes of any society whether contemporary or historical, whether a folk culture or a civilization.

This method of working with a short list of key terms to refer to a total context was adopted in order to overcome the difficulties in the way of comparing one society with another, or one cross-section of history or subcommunity with another. Unless an observer uses a list of key terms the same way in every context, it is impossible to be sure of valid comparisons. The observational standpoints—the bench marks —must be constant so that words will have a constant frame of reference. If a given term in the list were *not* used in referring to a given community we must be able to say that the phenomena were not there, or that they existed to an insignificant degree; not that the observer probably forgot to look, or that he looked and used a different word which he forgot to define.

The eight value categories define the culminating outcomes (values) toward which and from which we perceive that events in the social process are moving. All specialized terms in political analysis are definable in reference to the context whose basic features are thus characterized. When we describe particular patterns of practice specialized to the shaping and sharing of a value outcome, we are describing the "institutions" of a society. An institution is a pattern of "practices"; and a practice is a pattern of "perspectives" (symbols) and "operations." Taken in the aggregate all perspectives of an institution constitute its "myth"; all operations are its "technique."

Value List	*Institutions (examples)*
Power	Governments, political parties and orders, pressure groups and gangs
Wealth	Mines, plantations, farms, factories, offices, wholesaling, retailing, banking, consuming
Respect	Honor conferring (or stigmatizing) agencies; social class discriminations
Well-Being	Specialized facilities for safety, health, comfort
Rectitude	Agencies for setting and applying standards of responsibility; i.e., churches
Skill	Agencies for setting and applying standards of performance; i.e., professional associations, schools
Enlightenment	Mass and specialized media for obtaining, processing, disseminating and storing information
Affection	Intimate and congenial circles; identification with large groups

Outcomes (examples)

Decision	Electoral, legislative, administrative, judicial votes; victory or defeat in battle
Transaction	Pricing, bartering
Prestige	Giving or receiving prestige
Vitality	Giving or receiving aid in terms of psychosomatic integrity; giving or receiving damage
Rightness	Participating in the formulation of rules of responsibility; applying rules in concrete cases; serving as a target of rule application
Performance	Participation in the setting of performance standards; applications to concrete instances; serving as a target of application
Knowledge	Disclosing, withholding or receiving information about the past and estimates of the future
Cordiality	Conveying, withholding, or receiving affection (families, friendly circles); making or unmaking an identification with a larger group (national loyalty)

Politics deliberately refrained from restricting the proposed or assumed scope of political theory to any one category of value outcome. The accent was upon the validity of considering any participant in any social context in reference to any form of "influence" (a synonym for actual or potential value). One aim of the book was to disseminate a less trammelled conception of political analysis than the one generally current. If individual thinkers or groups of specialists prefer to carve out relatively restricted frames of reference, the map sketched in *Politics* provides a means of selecting and plotting the appropriate subdivisions.

The Strategy of Politics

The *Politics* had almost as much to say about the "How" as the "Who" and "What" of politics. Strategy is the management of value assets in order to influence outcomes. The base values (assets) at the disposal of any participant in politics depend upon his position in the social contexts to which he belongs. The value structure of any context, from the neighborhood to the globe, can be described in comparable terms by using the eight value categories outlined above. Since we usually find that each value is unequally distributed it is approximately correct to speak of value pyramids. But if communities are described in detail we often find more people occupying mid-positions than the top or bottom layers.

Strategies are classifiable according to the principal value that is being used to influence results. But we can cut down the number of categories by adopting a "horizontal" scheme that depends upon the relative degree of reliance placed upon symbols and resources. This is feasible because all activities necessarily use symbols and resources though in varying combinations.

When the manipulation of symbols was the subject of discussion in *Politics* the emphasis was upon their use to reach large groups. There are many ways of talking about this: "mass communication," "information," "psychological warfare (or 'peacefare')," "the ideological instrument of policy," and so on. Symbols are also prominent in the communications that pass among hostile, allied or neutral leaders; this is the diplomatic instrument employed in the negotiation of agreements. The accent is upon resources rather than symbols when the policy instrument is economic or when force is used. Attention is given to both instruments in *Politics*.

The fourfold division of policy instruments is particularly convenient when the external relations of a group are considered: information, diplomacy, economics, force (words, deals, goods, weapons). When we are examining the strategies used in the internal process of decision it is helpful to rely upon categories that make it easy to investigate the legal framework.

We look first for the organs authorized to lay down general rules in the name of the body politic. In democratic countries the most conspicuous organ relatively specialized to the *prescribing* function is a Congress or Parliament. Various organizations are authorized to *recommend* (promote) prescriptions, notably political parties. We note, too, that the *intelligence* function is provided for. The Chief Executive is usually charged with responsibility for factual reports and estimates of the future. The *invoking* function is exercised when prescriptions are applied to specific circumstances in a preliminary way as by policemen making arrests, grand juries issuing indictments, and tax officials circulating notices. The function of *application* is the "final" act within a total framework of prescription. For instance, it is the voice of a court. The *appraisal* function is performed by "auditors" and "supervisors." The *terminating* function is the responsibility of those who dissolve contractual or treaty obligations.

The seven categories can be used to analyze the formal arrangements of a legal code. They must be supplemented by proper methods of interviewing and direct observation before we can decide whether the facts of control match the forms of authority. Studies show that all functions are to some extent involved in the operations of every official organ, and that unofficial organizations (and individuals) often play the decisive part in the exercise of a given function. In the United States, for instance, the intelligence function is performed to a remarkable degree for voters and officials by the press.

The question that concerns a political strategist is how to manage the existing system to obtain favorable outcomes, and how to modify the system in order to affect future results. This issue was treated in the *Politics* when "Practices" were examined.

Not much was said about the aggregate patterns that emerge as the participants in a given arena act upon one another during the pre-outcome, outcome and post-outcome phases of decision. The most conspicuous fact is the shifting coalitions that appear in external or internal politics. This is the balancing of power.

One purpose of theories of strategy is to provide rational guidance to the participants in any arena of politics. Theories move in two directions and emphasize different parts of the same total act of choice. The first group of theories aims at improving the internal consistency of all explicit formulations. The second group is concerned with improving the procedures by which the validity of assumptions made in the first operation can be appraised.

Rational theories typically assume that the chooser is able to specify his preferred events under all the contingencies that would occur in an exhaustive map of expectation. The leading game theorist, von Neumann, not only provided an elegant mathematical proof of certain theorems of choice, but proposed an ingenious conception of "mixed strategies" designed to protect the strategist from disclosure of information to a rival. According to the rules of mixed strategy the decision maker leaves the final selection among alternatives to chance.

Decision theories of the second group proceed from the observation that individuals are hazy about the entire range of their demands and expectations, and that a crucial problem is how to enable the chooser to discover his "preference map." It is conceded that the experience of trying to act in accord with the advice given by the first group can, though under unknown conditions, improve the discovery process. Herbert Simon has recently proposed a formal theory intended to bridge the gap between the two emphases.

Both groups of theories consider the strategical problems that confront a single participant in an arena of varied composition. They also view the aggregate process in an arena in order to evaluate the pay-offs for all concerned.

Principles of strategy are formulated in action terms: *if* you want to accomplish *x*, do *y*. This economical mode of communication appeals to decision makers. It does, however, obscure the fact that "principles" can be re-stated in the form of propositions to be treated as scientific hypotheses for further research.

The Scientific Frame of Reference

Although *Politics* made use of available scientific studies and put forward hypotheses to be investigated further, it was not within the plan of the work to outline a body of basic and comprehensive propositions about the factors whose interaction is the political process. (To some extent this has been done subsequently.)

The scientific mode of thinking proceeds by formulating a theoretical model of how selected factors condition one another, and confronts the theory with observable "reality." The most comprehensive theories seek to explain the conditions under which one outcome is preferred over another and is in fact achieved. It is essential to distinguish between subjective events of "preference" and outcomes actually "achieved," since objectives are often pursued and remain unattained. The factors contributing to this disparity must be included in a comprehensive explanation of decision. It is also true that the objectives sought in a given situation are often viewed as "second choices" by those who make them. This implies that when the strategist calculated the net result of the alternatives perceived as open to him he concluded that the outcome which was "preferable in general" was not the one most preferable in the context.

A further point about conscious preferences and

volitions is that they are affected by unconscious factors which must also be taken into account by inclusive political theories.

It is to be noticed that participants are not only isolated individuals acting on their own, but groups of individuals acting together in varying degree as pressure groups, parties, government organs and the like. Theories of decision must also account for the demands and expectations made in the name of collectivities.

The political process can be analyzed with all its complexity if the value-institution analysis is fully applied. We think of politics in terms of *participants* (with identifications, demands, expectations; with control over base values) interacting in *arenas* (situations in which decision outcomes are expected) employing *strategies* to maximize value indulgences over deprivations by influencing *decision outcomes* and hence *effects*.

An advance in the contextual analysis of political strategy is the technique of discovering and accounting for the "operational code" of political participants which has been developed by Nathan Leites.

The configurative approach to political phenomena provides guidance for the scholar and scientist. With proper orientation they cannot fail to recognize that one of their principal tasks is to develop a comprehensive and selective intelligence function for themselves and others. Employing the value categories they will encourage *continuing surveys* of significant trends in "who gets what." Ideally they will consider the local community, the state, the nation and the globe; and estimate the degree of coverage that can be obtained at what cost (cost, that is, in terms of all values, not only dollars). They instigate whatever official or unofficial action is necessary to achieve a specified level of coverage.

The political scientist also takes *direct responsibility* for gathering facts. First come details of what is conventionally called government and politics. By "conventional" is meant local usage. In the United States, for instance, there is no problem in identifying the institutional practices of "governments," "political parties," or "pressure groups." Government also includes "laws" enacted by legislatures, "regulations" of executives and commissions, "decisions" of courts. Comprehended are all "votes" by electorates, legislatures, single executives, commissions, courts.

It is of obvious utility to have summaries on hand that show the history of the enactment and repeal of the formal prescriptions passed by legislatures and other official agencies, and of court decisions. But such summaries do not tell us whether the words found in statutes and ordinances are in fact put into effect. In short, knowledge of the words of a statute is not enough to tell us whether we have a law on a subject or not. It is of no advantage to conceive of "law" as solely consisting of language since political science and jurisprudence quite properly regard themselves as more than branches of linguistics. By law we mean authoritative language plus application (authority and control).

The task of discovering the effective legal code of a given body politic is, of course, a research enterprise of great scope. Obviously, reliance must be put upon more complex methods than reading printed statutes in a library. Studies can paint a picture of the way in which conventional institutions of government are functionally tied into the whole social context. The functional conception of politics, we have implied, refers to the definitions employed by scientific observers in order to make cultural comparisons. We, of course, define politics, law and government as institutions specialized to the making of the important decisions in a social context. What decision outcomes are important? Those which are expected to be, and are when necessary, made effective against challengers by the use of severe deprivations (sanctions). What sanctions are severe rather than mild? Those perceived as such by the members of the communities involved. Decisions are also matched according to the degree in which the whole community is implicated and the magnitude of the values at stake.

It is evident that no final conclusion can be drawn about the functional facts of a body politic until all the value-institution processes in a social context have been examined. Even this brief indication of the facts which the specialized student of politics has an obligation to encourage or supply makes it apparent that thousands of scholars are needed to maintain programs of investigation throughout the globe. Although no one individual can hope to have an exhaustive map of the whole, modern methods of processing data make it practicable for the first time to conceive of images of the whole that are based on vast collections of contemporary and historical data kept up to the moment by prompt computation.

More than knowledge of trends is to be included in the continuing self-survey of the process of world decision. It is essential to go as far as possible in the direction of keeping two levels of scientific knowledge up to date: first, correlations of trends occurring in a given context with all significant determining factors; second, summaries of the degree to which the basic propositions of political science are at present verified by available data.

Goals and Alternatives

Politics was concerned with sketching a "general physiology" of the political process rather than working out the strategies appropriate to any postulated system of public order. This task was deferred (and in part has been dealt with since). The biological sciences have policy branches, one of which is organized knowledge in reference to health ("medicine"). Another is "biological warfare" whose chief aim is incapacitation of enemies. Political science has policy branches suggested by such phrases as "the political science (or policy science) of democracy" or of despotism. In so far as the science of politics is a biological science it, too, includes policy sciences of death as well as of life.

New Haven, April, 1958

BIBLIOGRAPHICAL NOTES

CHAPTER ONE

The analysis of politics which is found in this book was briefly stated in the author's *World Politics and Personal Insecurity*, New York, 1935, Chap. 1, "The Configurative Method." Charles E. Merriam has been particularly influential in redefining the scope of political science in the United States. See *Political Power; Its Composition and Incidence*, New York, 1934. See also the works of Charles A. Beard. Among the younger writers reference may be made to G. E. G. Catlin, *The Science and Method of Politics*, New York, 1927, and Frederick L. Schuman, *International Politics; An Introduction to the Western State System*, New York, 1933, Chap. XIII. Similar formulations by European writers are not uncommon; see, in particular, Gaetano Mosca, *Elementi di scienza politica*, 2d ed., Turin, 1923; Max Weber, "Wirtschaft und Gesellschaft," in *Grundriss der Sozialökonomik*, III Abteilung, Tübingen, 1925; Part 1, Chap. 3; Part 2, Chap. 7; Part 3, Chaps. 1-11 incl. For data about the affiliations and successions of elites, see Pitirim Sorokin, *Social Mobility*, New

York, 1927; Vilfredo Pareto, *The Mind and Society*, 4 vols., New York, 1935; Roberto Michels, *Umschichtungen in den herrschenden Klassen nach dem Kriege*, Stuttgart, 1934. Data on the United States are in *Recent Economic Changes*, 2 vols., New York, 1929; *Recent Social Trends*, 2 vols., New York, 1933; Arthur N. Holcombe, *The New Party Politics*, New York, 1933; and *The Political Parties of Today*, 2d ed., New York, 1925.

CHAPTER TWO

For detailed references consult *Propaganda and Promotional Activities: An Annotated Bibliography*, compiled by H. D. Lasswell, R. D. Casey, and B. L. Smith, Minneapolis, 1935. On the general categories of myth, ideology, utopia, see Georges Sorel, *Réflexions sur la violence*, Paris, 1908; Karl Mannheim, *Ideologie und Utopie*, Bonn, 1929. For the inculcation of patriotism and the spread of nationalism, see Charles E. Merriam, *The Making of Citizens: A Comparative Study of Methods of Civil Training*, Chicago, 1931, summary volume of the "Civil Training Series," which contains monographs on the Soviet Union, Italy, Germany, Switzerland, France, the Dual Monarchy, Great Britain, United States, and primitive societies. For the new Germany, see Frederick L. Schuman, *The Nazi Dictatorship*, New York, 1935. For Italy, Herman Finer, *Mussolini's Italy*, New York, 1935. In this chapter I have drawn upon my article, "The Psychology of Hitlerism," *Political Quarterly*, 4:373-384 (July-September, 1933). The nature and effect of Entente propaganda against Germany are appraised in Hans Thimme, *Weltkrieg ohne Waffen*, Stuttgart, 1932. Propaganda to win and retain foreign aid is studied in Francis P. Renaut, *La politique de propagande des Américains durant la guerre d'indépendance*, 2 vols., Paris, 1922—. For revolutionary propaganda, Lenin, *What Is To Be Done?*, New York, 1928. For general propaganda in the United States, see E. P. Herring, Jr., *Group Representation before Congress*, Baltimore, 1929; *Public Administration and the Public Interest*, New York, 1936. A theory of propaganda is stated by Leonard W. Doob, *Propaganda: Its Psychology and Technique*, New York, 1935. In general consult Hardwood L. Childs, ed., "Pressure Groups and Propaganda," *Annals*, May, 1935.

CHAPTER THREE

On war, consult Quincy Wright, *The Causes of War and the Conditions of Peace*, London, New York, Toronto, 1935; Pitirim Sorokin, *Contemporary Sociological Theories*, Chap. VI, New York, 1928. S. Rudolf Steinmetz, *Soziologie des Krieges*, Leipzig, 1929. An early discussion of strategy and tactics is *The Book of War: The Military Classic of the Far East*, London, 1908. See Carl von Clausewitz, *Vom Kriege*, 3 vols., Berlin, 1832-1834. A recent brief treatise is by Sir Frederick B. Maurice, *Principles of Strategy*, New York, 1930. For separate aspects, refer to Adolf Caspary, *Wirtschaftsstrategie und Kriegsführung*, Berlin, 1932; Richard W. Rowan, *Spy and Counterspy; The Development of Modern Espionage*, New York, 1928; Maximilian Longe, *Kriegs- und Industrie-Espionage*, Vienna, 1930; H. D. Lasswell, *Propaganda Technique in the World War*, London and New York, 1927. Concerning police: Raymond B. Fosdick, *American Police Systems*, New York, 1920, and *European Police Systems*, New York, 1915; A. T. Vassilyev, *The Ochrana, the Russian Secret Police*, Philadelphia, 1930; Bruce Smith, *The State Police*, New York, 1925; J. P. Shalloo, *Private Police, with Special Reference to Pennsylvania*, Philadelphia, 1934; Edward Levinson, *I Break Strikes: The Technique of Pearl L. Bergoff*, New York, 1935. For the theory of armed revolutionary uprising, see A. Neuberg (pseud.), *Der bewaffnete Aufstand: Versuch einer theoretischen Darstellung*, Zurich, 1928 (secret literature of the Third International; imprint false). For the theory of assassination, see Netschajeff, *The Diary of a Revolutionist*.

CHAPTER FOUR

Case studies of rationing systems during the World War are to be found in Carnegie Endowment for International Peace, Division of Economics and History, *Economic and Social History of the World War*, ed. by James T. Shotwell. The conditions under which prices might be set by free competition are formulated in Frank H. Knight, *Risk, Uncertainty and Profit*, Boston, 1921. Studies of deviation from "perfect competition" are in such volumes as Erich

Egner, *Der Sinn des Monopols*, Berlin, 1931; J. M. Clark, *The Social Control of Business*, Chicago, 1926; D. M. Keezer and Stacy May, *The Public Control of Business*, New York, 1930; A. Salz, *Macht und Wirtschaftsgesetz*, Leipzig, 1930. On the Soviet Union, consult Calvin B. Hoover, *The Economic Life of Soviet Russia*, New York, 1931; William Henry Chamberlin, *Russia's Iron Age*, Boston, 1934; Sidney and Beatrice Webb, *Soviet Communism*, New York, 1936. For certain aspects of modern economic developments, see A. A. Berle, Jr., and Gardiner C. Means, *The Modern Corporation and Private Property*, New York, 1932; A. A. Berle and V. J. Pederson, *Liquid Claims and National Wealth*, New York, 1934; Harold G. Moulton, *The Formation of Capital*, Washington, 1935; Henry C. Simons, *A Positive Program for Laissez-Faire*, Chicago, 1934; J. M. Clark, *Studies in the Economics of Overhead Costs*, Chicago, 1923. On commercial policy, consult Josef Gruntzel, *System der Handelspolitik*, 3d ed., Vienna, 1928. Also Eugene Staley, *War and the Private Investor*, New York, 1935, and R. G. Hawtrey, *Economic Aspects of Sovereignty*, London, 1930. For special aspects of withholding, see Ernest Theodore Hiller, *The Strike: A Study in Collective Action*, Chicago, 1928; Wilfred Harris Crook, *The General Strike: A Study of Labor's Tragic Weapon in Theory and Practice*, Chapel Hill, 1931; Evans Clark, ed., *Boycotts and Peace*, New York, 1932; Charles F. Remer and William B. Palmer, *A Study of Chinese Boycotts with Special Reference to their Economic Effectiveness*, Baltimore, 1933; Clarence M. Case, *Non-violent Coercion: A Study in Methods of Social Control*, New York, 1923.

CHAPTER FIVE

The non-Marxist literature on government and administration has tended to minimize the elite consequences of institutional practices by considering relative "efficiency" or by using universalistic terms like "liberty" or "obedience." The study of governmental practices in relation to the total context was greatly stimulated in English-speaking countries by Graham Wallas, *Human Nature in Politics*, London, 1908, *The Great Society*, London, 1914, *Our Social Heritage*, London, 1921, and *The Art of Thought*, London, 1926. See also Thurman W. Arnold, *The Symbols* of Government, New Haven, 1935; Jerome Frank, *Law and the Modern Mind*, New York, 1930; E. S. Robinson, *Law and the Lawyers*, New Haven, 1935; Huntington Cairns, *Law and the Social Sciences*, New York, 1935; William A. Robson, *Civilization and the Growth of Law*, New York, 1935; Roscoe Pound, *An Introduction to the Philosophy of Law*, New Haven, 1922; A. Leist, *Privatrecht und Kapitalismus in neunzehnten Jahrundert*, Tübingen, 1911; A. V. Dicey; *Lectures on the Relation between Law and Public Opinion in England during the Nineteenth Century*, 2d ed., London, 1914; M. M. Bigelow, and others, *Centralization and the Law*, Boston, 1906. See also Harold J. Laski, *A Grammar of Politics, Part II*, New Haven, 1925; R. M. MacIver, *The Modern State*, Oxford, 1926; Franz Oppenheimer, *The State*, Indianapolis, 1914; J. W. Garner, *Political Science and Government*, New York, 1928; Alfred Weber, *Ideen zur Staats- und Kultur-Soziologie*, Karlsruhe, 1927; Georg Jellinek, *Allgemeine Staatslehre*, 3d ed., Berlin, 1914; Rudolf Kjellén, *Grundriss zu einem System der Politik*, Leipzig, 1920; J. R. Seeley, *Introduction to Political Science*, London, 1896; J. W. Burgess, *Political Science and Constitutional Law*, 2 vols., Boston, 1890; Henry Sidgwick, *The Elements of Politics*, London, 1891; Robert H. Lowie, *The Origin of the State*, New York, 1927; W. C. MacLeod, *The Origin and History of Politics*, New York, 1931; Frank J. Goodnow, *Politics and Administration*, New York, 1900; Ernst Freund, *Administrative Powers over Persons and Property*, Chicago, 1928, and *Standards of American Legislation*, Chicago, 1917; W. F. Willoughby, *Principles of Public Administration*, Baltimore, 1927; Leonard D. White, *Introduction to the Study of Public Administration*, New York, 1926. For new approaches, see the articles by Underhill Moore and collaborators in *Yale Law Review*; also H. D. Lasswell and Gabriel Almond, "Twisting Relief Rules," *Personnel Journal*, 13:338-343 (April, 1935).

CHAPTER SIX

Data about the skills and affiliations of legislators are in Karl Braunias, *Das parlamentarische Wahlrecht: Ein Handbuch über die Bildung der gesetzgebenden Körperschaften in Europa*. 2 vols.. Berlin and Leipzig, 1932. Eminent figures in Germany are analyzed by Fritz Giese, "Die öfftenliche Persönlichkeit," Beiheft 44, *Zeitschrift für angewandte Psychologie*, Leipzig, 1928. In general, consult A. M. Carr-Saunders and P. A. Wilson, *The Professions*, Oxford, 1933. For engineers, see A. P. M. Fleming and H. J. Brocklehurst, *A History of Engineering*, London, 1925; for physical scientists, W. C. D. Dampier, *A History of Science and Its Relations with Philosophy and Religion*, Cambridge, England, 1929. For physicians, consult Arthur Newsholme, *International Studies on the Relation between the Private and the Official Practice of Medicine with Special Reference to the Prevention of Disease*, 3 vols., London, 1931. Priests: Alfred Bertholet, "Priesthood," *Encyclopaedia of the Social Sciences*. For chiefs, bureaucrats, civil servants: W. C. MacLeod, *The Origin and History of Politics*, New York, 1931; Max Weber, "Politik als Beruf," in *Gesammelte Politische Schriften*, Munich, 1921; A. A. Lefas, *L'état et les fonctionnaires*, Paris, 1913; O. H. von der Gablentz, "Industriebureaukratie," *Schmollers Jahrbuch*, 50 (1926): 539-572. Diplomats: Severus Clemens, *Der Beruf des Diplomaten*, Berlin, 1926; Dale A. Hartman, "British and American Ambassadors," *Economica*, 11 (1931): 328-341. Bargainers: Werner Sombart, *Des Bourgeois*, Munich, 1920; F. W. Taussig and C. S. Joslyn, *American Business Leaders*, New York, 1932. Teachers, philosophers, social scientists: Edward H. Reisner, *Historical Foundations of Modern Education*, New York, 1927; H. Rashdall, *The Universities of Europe in the Middle Ages*, 2 vols., Oxford, 1895; Gladys Bryson, "The Emergence of the Social Sciences from Moral Philosophy," *International Journal of Ethics*, XLII (1932): 304-323. Lawyers: Max Rumpf, *Anwalt und Anwaltstand: Eine rechtswissenschaftliche und rechtssoziologische Untersuchung*, Leipzig, 1926; H. D. Hazeltine, Max Radin, A. A. Berle, Jr., "Legal Profession and Legal Education," *Encyclopaedia of the Social Sciences*. Journalists: International Labour Office, "Conditions of Work and Life of Journalists," *Studies and Reports*, ser. L, No. 2, Geneva, 1928; G. Bourdon and others, *Le journalisme d'aujourd'hui*, Paris, 1931; H. D. Lasswell, "Research on the Distribution of Symbol Specialists," *Journalism Quarterly*, 12:146-157 (June, 1935).

CHAPTER SEVEN

For fuller details of the class analysis of politics, consult H. D. Lasswell, *World Politics and Personal Insecurity,* New York, 1935; Max Nomad, *Rebels and Renegades,* New York, 1932; V. Pareto, *Les systèmes socialistes,* Paris, 1902-1903; Hendryk de Man, *The Psychology of Socialism,* London, 1928; Werner Sombart, *Der proletarische Sozialismus,* 2 vols., Jena, 1924; L. L. Lorwin, *Labor and Internationalism,* New York, 1929; Roberto Michels, *Zur Sozialogie des Parteiwesens in der modernen Demokratie,* 2d ed., Leipzig, 1925; Julien Benda, *The Treason of the Intellectuals,* New York, 1928. An important historical analysis is Eugen Rosenstock, *Die europäischen Revolutionen,* Jena, 1931. On dialectical materialism, see Sidney Hook, *Towards the Understanding of Karl Marx,* New York, 1933; Georg Lukács, *Geschichte und Klassenbewusstsein,* Berlin, 1923; N. Bukharin, *Historical Materialism,* New York, 1925; N. Lenin, *Materialism and Empirio-criticism,* New York, 1927; Karl Kautsky, *Die materialistische Geschichtsauffassung,* 2 vols., Berlin, 1927; Heinrich Cunow, *Die marxsche Geschichts-Gesellschafts- und Staatstheorie,* 2 vols., 4th ed., Berlin, 1923; V. Adoratsky, *Dialectical Materialism,* New York, 1934. See also Guy Stanton Ford, ed., *Dictatorship in the Modern World,* Minneapolis, 1935, notably essays by Max Lerner, Ralph H. Lutz, J. Fred Rippy, Hans Kohn; Harwood L. Childs, ed., *Dictatorship and Propaganda,* Princeton, 1936, especially essays by Oscar Jászi, Fritz M. Marx, H. D. Lasswell; Hermann Kantorowicz, "Dictatorships" (with a bibliography by Alexander Elkin), *Politica,* No. 4, August, 1935, pp. 470-508; M. T. Florinsky, *World Revolution and the U.S.S.R.,* New York, 1933; Harold J. Laski, *The State in Theory and Practice,* New York, 1935.

CHAPTER EIGHT

Modern methods of intensive personality study range from the prolonged interview of Sigmund Freud, in which the subject indulges in free association, through various abbreviated interviews to the systematic observation of the acts of subjects who are unaware that they are being investigated. Recent literature is focusing attention upon the position of the observer in his field of reference; his abstract language is thus construed in terms of his characteristic method. An appreciation of the range of intensive approaches may be obtained by referring to the summary volume by Pauline V. Young, *Interviewing in Social Work*, New York, 1935. John Dollard has undertaken to formulate *Criteria for the Life History*, New Haven, 1935. Ways of objectifying the prolonged psychoanalytic interview are discussed in H. D. Lasswell, *Psychopathology and Politics*, Chap. XI, Chicago, 1930, and in subsequent articles in *Psychoanalytic Review* and *Imago* (Vienna). A succinct introduction to modern psychological conceptions is found in Bernard Hart, *Psychology of Insanity*, Cambridge, England, 1912. For general psychiatry, see William A. White, *Outline of Psychiatry*, 13th ed., Washington, 1932. Among influential authors, reference may be made to Sigmund Freud, Alfred Adler, and Carl Jung. Emphasis upon symbolic expressions in relation to biological traits is found in Ernst Kretschmer, *Textbook of Medical Psychology*, translated by E. B. Strauss, London, 1934. Current development in the various fields of psychology may be followed through the handbooks edited by Carl Murchison at the Clark University Press, Worcester, Mass. For typological or for individual studies of special interest to political scientists, reference may be made to Richard Behrendt, *Politischer Aktivismus, Ein Versuch zur Sociologie und Psychologie der Politik*, Leipzig, 1932; Fritz Künkel, *Grundzüge der politischen Charakterkunde*, Leipzig, 1933; Alexander Herzberg, *The Psychology of Philosophers*, New York, 1929; L. Pierce Clark, *Lincoln, A Psycho-Biography*, New York, 1933 (extensively used in this chapter); H. F. Gosnell, *Negro Politicians*, Chicago, 1935; John Gunther, *Inside Europe*, New York, 1936; Fedor Vergin, *Subconscious Europe*, London, 1932.

CHAPTER NINE

The analysis of specific attitudes is complicated by the fact that attitudes are influenced by other attitudes, as well as by material conditions. The psychological significance of the state is studied in Jacob Wackernagel, *Der Wert des Staates*, Basel, 1934. An elaborate research on the relation between the family and every form of authority is *Studien über Autorität und Familie*, Forschungsberichte aus dem Institut für Sozialforschung, Paris, 1936. Nationalism, nationality, and patriotism are probed from several standpoints in the writings of Charles E. Merriam, Hans Kohn, Carlton J. H. Hayes, Roberto Michels. See especially Heinz O. Ziegler, *Die moderne Nation; Ein Beitrag zur politischen Soziologie*, Tübingen, 1931. Concerning militant attitudes, consult Edward Glover, *War, Sadism and Pacifism*, London, 1933, and Robert Waelder, *Lettre sur l'étiologie et l'évolution des psychoses collectives*, Institut international de coopération intellectuel, 1933. For experiments on morale in modern industrial plants, consult Elton Mayo, *The Human Problems of an Industrial Civilization*, New York, 1933. An observational and interrogatory procedure for the study of positive and negative personal relations is found in J. L. Moreno, *Who Shall Survive? A New Approach to the Problem of Human Interrelations*, Washington, 1934. The psychological characterization of personality and culture is discussed in Ruth Benedict, *Patterns of Culture*, Boston, 1934. For an analysis of changing interrelationships, see H. D. Lasswell, "Collective Autism as a Consequence of Culture Contact," *Zeitschrift für Sozialforschung*, IV (1935): 232-247. An analysis of assertiveness in response to deprivation is Gabriel Almond and H. D. Lasswell, "Aggressive Behavior by Clients Toward Public Relief Administrators: A Configurative Analysis," *American Political Science Review*, XXVIII (1934): 643-655. On certain aspects of proletarian socialism, consult *Die Organization im Klassenkampf. Die Probleme der Arbeiterklasse*, Berlin, 1932, notably the essay by Fritz Bieligk. For the relation between changing collective attitudes and law, consult Svend Ranulf, *The Jealousy of the Gods and Criminal Law at Athens: A Contribution to the Sociology of Moral Indignation*, 2 vols., London and Copenhagen, 1933-1934; Jerome Hall, *Theft, Law and Society*, Boston, 1935.

CHAPTER TEN

On developments in the United States: Lewis Corey, *The Crisis of the Middle Class*, New York, 1935; Alfred Bingham, *Insurgent America: Revolt of the Middle Classes*, New York, 1935; Lawrence Dennis, *Coming American Fascism*, New York, 1936; "The Unofficial Observer" (pseud.), *American Messiahs*, New York, 1935; Raymond Gram Swing, *Forerunners of American Fascism*, New York, 1935; William Yandell Elliott, *The Need for Constitutional Reform*, New York, 1935; and especially T. V. Smith, *The Promise of American Politics*, Chicago, 1936. As for functional groups, there are a number of scattered publications on trade associations, federations of labor, farm organizations, etc. On devices of mixed government and private control, see Sidney and Beatrice Webb, *A Constitution for the Socialist Commonwealth of Great Britain*, London and New York, 1920; Harold A. Van Dorn, *Government Owned Corporations*, New York, 1926; Marshall E. Dimock, *British Public Utilities and National Development*, London, 1933, and *Government-Operated Enterprises in the Panama Canal Zone*, Chicago, 1934; Marquis Childs, *Sweden: The Middle Way*, New Haven, 1936; Kurt Wiedenfeld, "Wesen und Bedeutung der gemischt-wirtschaftlichen Unternehmung," in *Schmollers Jahrbuch* 55: 439-456 (1931); Julius Landmann, ed., *Moderne Organisationsformen der öffentlichen Unternehmungen*, Schriften des Vereins für Sozialpolitik, pt. 2, vol. 176, Munich, 1931; "Government Owned Corporations," *Encyclopaedia of the Social Sciences* (by Paul Webbink). On corporation forms, see James C. Bonbright and Gardiner C. Means, *The Holding Company; Its Public Significance and Its Regulation*, New York, 1932; Eliot Jones, *The Trust Problem in the United States*, New York, 1921; Robert Liefmann, *Die Unternehmungsformen*, 4th ed., Stuttgart, 1930.

Harold Lasswell, one of the few major creative figures in modern political science, is associated with the Yale Law School. Besides *Politics,* he is the author of several other seminal works in political theory: *Psychopathology and Politics* (1930), *World Politics and Personal Insecurity* (1935; republished in 1950) and *Democratic Character* (1951). All of the aforementioned works are published by The Free Press. In addition to them, however, Professor Lasswell is a frequent contributor to scholarly journals and numerous other works on the problems of power, status, and elites.